LORD, What's Really Important?

Fritz Ridenour

A Division of G/L Publications GL Regal Books
Glendale, California, U.S.A.

Other good Regal reading:
Candid Questions About Morality
  by J. Edwin Orr
Issues and Answers
  by Gary Maeder with Don Williams
Strategy for Living
  by Edward R. Dayton and Ted W. Engstrom

Scripture quotations in this publication, unless otherwise
indicated, are from the *New American Standard Bible* © The
Lockman Foundation 1960, 1962, 1963, 1968, 1971. Used by
permission.
Other versions quoted are:
TLB From *The Living Bible*, Copyright © 1971 by Tyndale House
Publishers, Wheaton, Illinois. Used by permission.
Phillips The New Testament in Modern English, Revised Edition,
J.B. Phillips, Translator. © J.B. Phillips 1958, 1960, 1972. Used
by permission of Macmillan Publishing Co., Inc.
NIV New International Version. New Testament. Copyright © 1973 by
New York Bible Society International. Used by permission.
JB The Jerusalem Bible. Copyright © 1966, 1967 and 1968 by
Darton, Longman & Todd Ltd. and Doubleday & Company, Inc.
KJV Authorized King James Version
AMP Amplified Bible, The. Copyright © 1962, 1964 by Zondervan
Publishing House. Used by permission.

Published by Regal Books Division, G/L Publications
Glendale, California 91209
Printed in U.S.A.

Library of Congress Catalog Card No. 78-58945
ISBN 0-8307-0622-3

CONTENTS

Values are Lived, Not Recited

This has been a challenging book to write. For one thing, a subject like values is hard to focus. Ask 10 people their definition of values and you will get 10 different answers. Ask for a definition of Christian values and it gets worse. I am waiting for someone to tell me "A Christian value is a church where you get your money's worth!"

So, right at the start, to explain what I mean by "values" in this book:

Values—the things, beliefs or people that are really important to you, so important that they affect what you do, say and how you live.

Another way to say it might be: "Your values are your life-style." We have certain Christian beliefs and doctrines. But by simply reciting the Apostles' Creed or the Ten Commandments we cannot say, "*these* are my values." You live your values, you don't recite them.

For example, try spending some time with another

person. Do things together and talk together. Compete with one another in some kind of game or sport. Both of you will soon have a much better picture of each other's real values.

Another thing that makes a book like this difficult is the sticky question: "How do we get—and keep—the 'right' values?" We all have different standards, different ideas of what is really important. Who is to say what is "right"?

Most of today's secular educators are humanistic in their approach to values. Values specialists like Sidney Simon claim that values can't really be transferred or passed on to the next generation. Schools, churches, heroes, models, good examples, etc., have all failed to do so. Instead of trying to transfer values, says Simon, we can only help people learn to clarify or identify the values they have already.[1]

While I appreciate the thinking and work of Simon and other values specialists,[2] I don't agree with their premise that values can't be transferred. Jesus didn't agree either, as a look at His teachings will quickly show you. Whatever criticisms can be made of organized Christianity, the undeniable fact is that *something* has been transmitted for almost 2,000 years that has to go by the general title of "Christian values."

It should be noted here that there is quite a bit more to Christianity than transmitting a system of doctrine. The Bible is far more than a collection of teachings and other Jewish literature. All Scripture is given by inspiration of God, it does not come from someone's private opinion (or values, see 2 Tim. 3:16; 2 Pet. 1:20,21).

There is only one possible source to which the Christian can turn to learn the "right values." That source is God, whom we know through His Word, living and written.[3] So, in this book we will let the Bible—especial-

6

ly the teachings of Jesus—be our base of authority and our source for finding principles to live by. Note that I said "principles," not rules or regulations. The worst mistake we can make is to try to reduce Christian values to a list of proof texts. There is a big difference between making God's Word your source of authority and forcing it to become a rule book for every situation. The first time we hit something the Bible doesn't refer to specifically (abortion, for example), we're stuck.

I'm also making the assumption that if you're bothering to read this book, you're a Christian, or at least you're interested in what a Christian is and does. In each major section we will take a look at a problem or question that concerns most Christians. Then we'll see what Jesus had to say about it and how we can apply the principles He taught in the first century to our particular situation in the twentieth.

To help you apply Jesus' teachings to your life in today's world I have also included brief, easy-to-do questionnaires and quizzes that will help you see how much you value certain beliefs, ideas, people or things. What is really important to you? You may be surprised by some of your own answers.

There is also plenty of "how-to" material—practical suggestions on how to strengthen or start changing your values. We don't change our values overnight; they are part of our habits, our life-style. It's never easy to break a bad habit or form a new and positive one. But to paraphrase that old Chinese saying about getting started on a thousand-mile trip, "Journey toward more Christ-centered values begins with small steps." Some ideas for taking those first small steps are there if you want to use them. Better yet, the Holy Spirit may give you your own ideas for improving your life. And those are the best kinds of all.

Obviously no one book can cover every problem or question, but I do hope to make a start on helping us think about something that is absolutely crucial in everyone's life—values. Reduced to the bare minimum, values are what we feel is important. And what we feel is important is what drives us to do (or not do) certain things.

Values are what drove the hero of the film *Rocky* to go the distance and take grueling punishment at the hands of the heavyweight champion of the world.

Values are what caused one group of youths to shoot an ice cream vendor when he refused their demands for money. And values are what caused some bystanders to rush to the man's aid, while others, ranging in age from very young to near adult, raided the truck and carried off an undetermined amount of ice cream.[4]

Values are what cause a girl and a guy to "live together" without a marriage commitment. Values turn one man into a missionary, another into a hijacker of airliners. Values are why the psalmist wrote from captivity in Babylon: "Jerusalem, if I forget you, may my right hand wither!" (Ps. 137:5, *JB*).

There are all kinds of values that can be a part of anyone's life, and there is a lot of disagreement in this world about which values are the right ones to hold. Every Christian, however, faces a basic question: Are my values what they should be? Am I living according to the teachings of Christ and the Bible? Those aren't easy questions, but the answers are there—if we're not afraid to look.

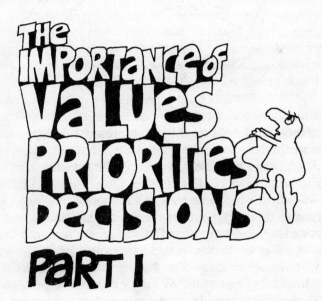

The IMPORTANCE of VALUES PRIORITIES DECISIONS

PART I

1. The World's Mold—A Perfect Fit?
2. How to Battle the "Big Squeeze"
3. First Things Second?
4. A Plan for Straightening Out Priorities
5. Not to Decide—Is Impossible!
6. How Can I Make Better Decisions?

CHAPTER 1

THE WORLD'S MOLD— a PERFECT FIT?

"How can I cope in this huge pressure cooker called the world?"

Just about everybody is asking that question, including most of us who call ourselves Christians. In fact, life in the world's pressure cooker has special challenge and meaning to every believer. Being a Christian is not always easy. God's grace and salvation are free, but there is a daily price to pay called "trust and obey."

Christians are taught to walk a fine line labeled "*in* the world, but not *of* it." We are expected to perform— raise our kids, earn the high salary, keep the yard decent, pay our bills and taxes. In general, we are supposed to operate successfully in a success-oriented world.

But, at the same time Christians are supposed to stay on center spiritually. Our values should never allow concerns about money, popularity, position, status, etc., to come between us and Christ. As J.B. Phillips so aptly translates Romans 12:2, we are to guard against letting the world squeeze us into its own mold.

And squeeze us the world does. In fact, "worldliness" is a good candidate for Top Temptation of this or any other year. The trouble is we don't really believe this. We are so busy running the daily rat race we don't always notice how we are conforming more and more to worldly values and standards. In fact, there are so many goodies to enjoy, so many fantastic things to try, that the world's mold slips on quite nicely. We don't even get the sensation of being squeezed. It's a perfect fit.[1]

How Television Bathes Your Brain

One of the best examples of how the worldly mold can gently squeeze your mind is television. Without question, television has tremendous potential for good. It has brought entertainment, learning and information to millions of people who would be the poorer without it. But television has also brought scenes of violence, immoral sex, cheating, robbery, rape and mayhem into the homes of families around the world. In addition, television bathes our brains daily with enticing pitches designed to tell us what to buy, what to do, what to believe. There is no single communicator of worldly values with more power than television.

Key to American television programming is the Almighty Buck. Nielsen ratings decide the fate of each show and sponsors call the tune. Sometimes it's hard to tell the programs from the ads. (Sometimes the ads are better.)

As for the basic TV programming menu, it varies little from season to season. Worthwhile shows like "60 Minutes," "The Waltons," "Wide World of Sports," "Little House on the Prairie," and the screening of Alex Haley's "Roots" are heavily outweighed by the usual

11

fare of banality, heavily spiced with violence or sex.

Every new season finds its latest "test case" to see how far the networks can go. In the fall of 1977 the big test was "Soap"—a sort of spoof on the depressive jungle of daytime soap operas that have run on TV for years. Despite early outcries from many groups and individuals, ABC weathered the storm and so did "Soap," which eventually settled in to gain a hefty share of the Nielsen ratings. But "Soap" didn't fool the critics, who recognized it for the slick piece of trash it was. And what exactly was wrong with "Soap"? Why did Cecil Smith of the *Los Angeles Times* call it "a prolonged dirty joke"?

Mainly because almost everybody in the show was on the make, including a mother and her teenage daughter who were both having an affair with the same tennis pro. (In the opening episode the mother left the tennis pro's bedroom by one door as her daughter knocked at the other.)

Other features in "Soap" included the bumbling antics of a young hood who had connections with organized crime. The mob ordered him to kill his stepfather, who, by the way, had killed his wife's first husband in order to marry her and who, by the way, was suffering from impotency due to guilt feelings and who, by the way, was continually being shocked by his homosexual stepson who, by the way ... anyway, you get the very soapy, yet dirty, picture.

The Real Danger in "Soap"

What makes shows like "Soap" so dangerous is that they are fast paced, entertaining and, in spots, downright amusing. The result is that the viewer is lured into thinking that fornication, adultery, homosexuality and even murder are all just a joke, just good clean innocent fun that "deals with human behavior as it actually is."[2] The joke, of course, is on the public, as the networks and sponsors of shows like "Soap" clean up while taking hilarious trips to the bank.

Shows like "Soap," "Three's Company," and "Love American Style" are all designed to make the worldly mold fit ever so snug. Even a show like "James at 15," which was acclaimed by critics in its opening weeks during the fall 1977 season, still sold the typical message of the new morality and situation ethics: "Do what you want to do, just be sure it's loving and right."

In mid-season James turned 16 and received as a "present" the loss of his virginity with Chris, a beautiful Swedish exchange student. One TV critic went to great lengths (about 19 column-inches in the *Los Angeles Times*) to assure his readers that the flowering of fornicative passion between James and Chris was "—a charming play, tender and funny and marvelously aware of the thoughts and attitudes of contemporary youth. There's even a discussion of birth control prior to the romantic moment."[3]

What Did Jesus Say About Values?

Television, newspapers and magazines were not around when Jesus walked the dusty roads of Palestine with His disciples. Did He have any concerns about His followers getting squeezed into the worldly mold? Indeed He did and nowhere did He make it clearer than about halfway through the Sermon on the Mount.

Conditions were different when Jesus taught His Sermon on the Mount, but people were the same then as they are now. Jesus wanted to warn us against a way of thinking that could easily ruin our relationship to Him. This attitude can take two forms: (1) You can just out and out love the things and experiences this world of-

13

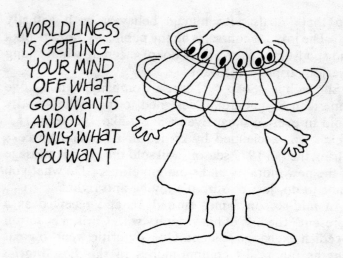

WORLDLINESS IS GETTING YOUR MIND OFF WHAT GOD WANTS AND ON ONLY WHAT YOU WANT

fers; (2) You can spend a great deal of your time being anxious about having enough of the world's goods to "make it."[4] Either way the devil has your mind *off what God wants* and on *what you want*, which is precisely what happened to Adam and Eve in the garden. The result was the Fall, and the whole human race has been a sucker for worldliness ever since. It's not surprising that Jesus said:

> *Do not lay up for yourselves treasures upon earth, where moth and rust destroy, and where thieves break in and steal; but lay up for yourselves treasures in heaven, where neither moth nor rust destroys, and where thieves do not break in or steal; for where your treasure is, there will your heart be also* (Matt. 6:19-21).

When Jesus talked about "laying up treasures on earth," He described three basic sources of wealth in Palestine: *clothing* or fine fabrics; *food*, especially grain; and *money*, silver and gold. Jesus reminded His listeners that none of these items could last. Fine fabrics could be destroyed by moths. In verse 19, the Greek word translated "rust" is *brosis*, which means "to eat away." Jesus knew that grain and other goods could be eaten by mice, rats, locusts, grasshoppers, etc. And, of course, thieves could always break in and steal one's possessions. In Palestine at that time "breaking in" wasn't done with jimmies or lock picks. Thieves waited until the homeowner was gone and then literally broke right through the clay walls of the house![5]

What Jesus was saying is that nothing in this world is permanent. It can be destroyed; it can wear out; it can be stolen. Ultimately, He was warning against more than accumulating money and things. Earthly treasures can include people, popularity, status, glory—anything that comes first in our lives. He was talking about a value system turned upside down, where the less important is put ahead of the really important.

We can see this today in our own society where entertainers are paid far larger salaries than are civic leaders, doctors, lawyers, preachers and teachers. One cartoonist summed it up nicely when he showed two old ladies talking. Said one: "Isn't it a shame? They signed a baseball player to a salary higher than the President's!" The other replied: "Why not? He had a better year!"[6]

What, Then, Are Treasures in Heaven?

No matter how great your fame, wealth or achievements, treasures on earth are never enough to satisfy. On the other hand, says Jesus, you can lay up treasures in heaven, which never wear out, never get eaten or stolen. What does He mean?

The treasure in heaven most Christians think of first is salvation, and certainly Jesus was talking about that. But He was also thinking about living the kind of life God wants us to live. Later in the sixth chapter of Mat-

15

thew, Jesus described this kind of living as seeking first the Kingdom of God and His righteousness (see Matt. 6:33). How well Christians do this kind of seeking determines their character, their view of life, the inner qualities that make them who they are.

During the Decian persecution of the Christians in A.D. 286, Roman soldiers broke into a Christian church and demanded that Laurentius, the deacon, show them the church's treasures. Laurentius pointed to the hungry being fed, the sick being cared for and said, "*These* are the treasures of the Church."[7]

A rather grim Spanish proverb says: "There are no pockets in a shroud." In other words, when you die you carry nothing from this world but *you*. Your body is left behind. If all your interests have been *here* (on earth) you won't be ready for *there* (heaven).

It's no wonder Jesus points out that where your treasure is, there will your heart be also. No verse in the entire Bible sums up Christian values better than this. Whatever you consider truly important is what captures your time, energy, heart and mind.

What do we think about most? Where do we spend our time and what do we do with it, especially the leisure hours?

How Clean Are Your Windows?

As Jesus continues He gives another valuable tip on how to resist being squeezed into the world's own mold:

The lamp of the body is the eye; if therefore your eye is clear, your whole body will be full of light. But if your eye is bad, your whole body will be full of darkness. If therefore the light that is in you is darkness, how great is the darkness! (Matt. 6:22,23).

Jesus is using symbolism and imagery here to teach

16

something very important. He is saying that your eye—how you look at things—is the window of your soul. The cleaner the window, the more light that comes in. If your eye is clear—if you are living in a way that lays up treasures in heaven—you will be full of light. But if your eye is clouded and begrimed by materialism, pride, conceit, selfishness, greed, etc., you will be full of spiritual darkness. "And oh, how *deep* that darkness can be!" (Matt. 6:23, *TLB*).

Serve God or???

To clinch the whole thing Jesus adds one more thought:

> *No one can serve two masters; for either he will hate the one and love the other .... You cannot serve God and Mammon* (Matt. 6:24).

These are plain words. When it comes to following Christ you have a clear choice. You can serve Him or you can serve Mammon, which is also translated "money" or "material things." You can be His disciple or you can be squeezed into the world's own mold.

When Jesus used the word "Mammon" He knew just what kind of impact it would have on His listeners. There had been a time in the past when mammon had meant "something to be entrusted to someone who would keep it safe." But by the time Jesus walked the earth Mammon was spelled with a capital "M" and had come to mean "that in which I put my trust." In other words, Mammon was no less than a god.[8]

It's surprising what can become gods in our lives—those things that crowd out the real God or at least leave Him very little of our time or interests. Theologian Harvey Cox describes one of today's biggest fads, which is not worshiping things or possessions but worshiping experience. This new kind of gluttony "transforms the entire range of human ideas and emotions into a well-stocked pantry. Today, only the old-fashioned glutton still stuffs his mouth with too many entrees. The new glutton craves experience: in quantity and variety, more and better, increasingly exotic, and even spiritual.

"Today's money does not lust after houses, cars and clothes, but travel, drugs, unusual sights and sounds, exotic tastes, therapies, and new emotional states. If disgrace haunts the affluent it is not apt to be for failing to *have* something but rather for failing to have *tried* something."[9]

Having too much or trying too much—it all adds up to serving Mammon instead of God. It is easy to get defensive about how we spend our time and money. We scream "legalism!" if anyone questions our particular life-style under God's grace. Or we chuckle and shrug off the spiritual naivete in worrying about "getting too worldly." But as the secular system clasps us in fond embrace we may do well to take stock:

WHERE YOUR VALUES ARE
THERE WILL YOUR HEART BE ALSO.

CHAPTER 2
HOW TO BATTLE THE BIG SQUEEZE

So far we have established a couple of basic things:
First, the world's mold is pressing in on Christians harder yet more subtly than ever before.

Second, Jesus knew what the world could do to a Christian and He warned us against it. Where our treasure is, there will our hearts be also. We cannot serve God and Mammon (materialism).

So how do we apply Jesus' words to where we are today? Are we to flee the world? Become ascetics or hermits who have nothing to do with anyone? Should we live like a modern day Simeon Stylites, sitting at the top of a pole and never coming down?

And how can we find the "right" values? Is it even possible?

As we have already seen, values are hard to pin down. Still, we are quite certain there is a real difference between earthly (worldly) values and heavenly (spiritual) ones. One way to start discovering and living the "right" values is to see how our own ideas and opinions match up with what Jesus said about laying up treasures in heaven and serving God instead of Mammon (see Matt. 6:19-24).

Take a Look at Your Values

For example, on a scale of 1 to 10 where do your true interests lie regarding the following?

• I work hardest at laying up

1	2	3	4	5	6	7	8	9	10

treasures   treasures
on earth   in heaven

(Go ahead, be honest. And remember, marking the line right in the middle is a cop-out.)

• My life-style conforms more closely with

1	2	3	4	5	6	7	8	9	10

the world   God's will

(Mark where you actually are, not where you would like to be.)

• As I move through my usual weekly routine I find myself concerned with

1	2	3	4	5	6	7	8	9	10

Mammon   serving God
(material things)

(One way to think about this one is to estimate how often you bring God into your daily routine rather than just being swept along with the pressures, the schedules, the deadlines and "getting everything done.")

The major temptation when answering questions like those above is to fudge a little toward the spiritual side.

Ask these questions aloud in the typical Sunday School class and almost everyone will give answers that make him look like a "good Christian," or at least no worse than the rest. Keep in mind that as you answer each question in private you can be as honest as you can stand. It's difficult to be totally honest; sometimes we aren't even sure what "totally honest" is. On some days we might answer those three questions one way; on other days the answers would be quite different.

But, to get some value out of all this, try to think of your general pattern, what you usually do, who you usually associate with, what you usually say to family, friends or strangers.

Now that you've gotten the hang of it, try taking three more looks at your values:

● To me, money is

1	2	3	4	5	6	7	8	9	10

not very
important

supremely
important

(Nothing is trickier than money. We all want it; we all need it. The real question is: "Do I control my money, or does it control me?")

● As a rule I use my time

1	2	3	4	5	6	7	8	9	10

wastefully

wisely

(Careful on this one. Maybe you need to keep track of your time for a few days to see where it really goes. Nothing is more impossible to regain. Once wasted, time is gone forever.)

● I am using my mental and physical abilities at the rate of

1	2	3	4	5	6	7	8	9	10

very little

full capacity

(Psychologists pretty well agree that we use only a small percentage of our potential abilities. Another way of asking the question is, "Am I doing the *best* I can?")

When thinking about your values it's possible to take one of three approaches:

The ho-hum approach takes the attitude that "Well, my values are my values. I do pretty well. It's pretty hard to say where I am in regard to this stuff. There's no need to get in a stew."

The overwhelmed breathless approach says: "Good grief! There's just too much here to think about. It's all too big for me. I wouldn't know how to start carving this stuff down to size. I better just stand pat."

The happy medium approach, however, says this: "I know I'm not up to par with Jesus' values. Nobody is, but He loves me anyway in spite of my flaws. I'll pick one, maybe two or three things and work on them, with Christ's help."

So, go over your answers. Where can you start laying up more treasures in heaven, fewer on earth? In what specific way can you break out of the worldly mold and seek more of God's will? How can you start serving Mammon (material things) *less* and God *more*?

Some Ideas for Making Changes

Here are just a few starter ideas for specific steps you might take right now to change some of your values, strengthen others:

1. Pray daily, asking God to reveal to you where your values are weak or even just plain poor. Ask Him to help you change.

2. Do more Bible reading and study. There is more about values in the Bible than in any other book.

3. Try budgeting your money on the 10-80-10 plan

(give 10 percent to the Lord, live on 80 percent, put 10 percent in savings).

4. Try cutting TV watching time by 10 percent each week. For example, if you are watching 10 hours of television, cut it to nine and engage in some other constructive activity like reading, Bible study and prayer, talking to your spouse or kids, exercising, making macrame, or working on some other hobby. After you succeed at cutting 10 percent, try for 20 percent and possibly even more.

5. Try reaching out to others in a specific way. Is there someone you should write to? Someone you should go visit? Some service project or other ministry you should engage in? Someone to whom you should witness?

Those are just a few ideas; you can think of many more. The important thing is that whatever you choose, it's something you know *you* should do.

All of us can take positive steps toward better values. It's impossible to avoid the big squeeze applied by the world because we live in it daily. But we don't have to give in. We don't have to be molded into conformists who go along with wrong values just because everybody else is doing it or because it's just easier to get by that way. Following is a personal paraphrase of Romans 12:2 from the *Phillips* translation that you may want to memorize and repeat as a daily prayer:

LORD, I DON'T WANT THE WORLD
TO SQUEEZE ME INTO ITS MOLD.
REMOLD MY MIND FROM WITHIN
AND PROVE IN PRACTICE
THAT YOUR PLAN FOR ME IS GOOD,
THAT IT MEETS ALL YOUR SPECIFICATIONS
AND THAT IT MOVES ME TOWARD SPIRITUAL MATURITY.

CHapTeR 3
FIRST THINGS SECOND?

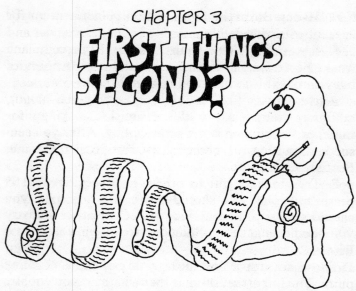

When talking about values you almost have to talk about priorities in the same breath. According to Webster, priorities are "an order of preference based on urgency, importance or merit." In other words, your priorities are things you choose to do before other things, because you want to or have to.

Your priorities are a nitty-gritty picture of how you are living out your values. If something is truly important to you, it will land high on your list of things to do, enjoy, use, etc.

One man's order of priorities made front page news late in 1977 when Jean Bedel Bokassa, a former French paratrooper, crowned himself emperor of the Central African Republic in a ceremony that cost *30 million dollars*. As part of the festivities Bokassa received a six-foot diamond-encrusted scepter, was draped in a 24-foot red velvet cloak, sat on a two-ton gold plated throne, shaped like a 15-foot high eagle.

Following Bokassa's coronation a gala reception for 2,000 guests included hundreds of pounds of caviar and 24,000 bottles of champagne, flown by chartered plane from Paris, as well as more than 250 luxury automobiles imported from Europe for use by Bokassa's guests.

As a comparatively new nation (founded in 1960), was the Central African Republic really ready for Bokassa's 30 million dollar blowout? It wouldn't seem so. Boasting a population of two million at that time, Bokassa's kingdom was listed as one of the world's 25 poorest countries, with an annual income of only $155 per person.[1] Yet Bokassa was quoted as saying, "One cannot create a great history without sacrifices."[2]

It would be simple enough to observe that Emperor Bokassa's priorities desperately need straightening out. Dozens of worthwhile things could have been built or purchased with the 30 million dollars. But it really doesn't help much to judge Emperor Bokassa. He is a rather extreme example of how one man set up his priorities. The question for us is: how should Christians set up *their* priorities in regard to money, time, activities?

What Did Jesus Say About "Priorities"?

If you think about it, most of Jesus' Sermon on the Mount and many of His other teachings deal with priorities. In the Beatitudes (Matt. 5:1-10) He talked about what to put first if you want to be happy.

He also talked about the importance of Christians being salt and light to the world (Matt. 5:13-16). He pointed out how important the law was and how He had come to fulfill it, not abolish it (Matt. 5:17-20).

He taught us how to give the right way (Matt. 6:1-4) and how to fast and pray (Matt. 6:5-18).

The list goes on and on, but there is a question. What did Jesus think was top priority of all? We find the answer in Matthew 6:25-33, where He begins by saying:

> For this reason I say to you, do not be anxious for your life, as to what you shall eat, or what you shall drink; nor for your body, as to what you shall put on. Is not life more than food, and the body than clothing? Look at the birds of the air, that they do not sow, neither do they reap, nor gather into barns; and yet your heavenly Father feeds them. Are you not worth much more than they? And which of you by being anxious can add a single cubit to his life's span?
>
> And why are you anxious about clothing? Observe how the lilies of the field grow; they do not toil nor do they spin, yet I say to you that even Solomon in all his glory did not clothe himself like one of these. But if God so arrays the grass of the field, which is alive today and tomorrow is thrown into the furnace, will He not much more do so for you, O men of little faith?
>
> Do not be anxious then, saying, "What shall we eat?" or "What shall we drink?" or "With what shall we clothe ourselves?" For all these things the Gentiles eagerly seek; for your heavenly Father knows that you need all these things (Matt. 6:25-32).

At first glance it might seem Jesus is suggesting that all Christians should go on welfare. Many people honestly need welfare assistance, but there are thousands who prefer to collect their welfare checks rather than take perfectly good jobs that are offered to them. Jesus isn't suggesting that we become freeloaders who don't want to work; essentially He is saying we shouldn't *worry* about what we will eat or drink or about what we will wear. Worry never helps; it doesn't add a thing and only takes away the joy in life.

For Jesus, concentrating on material things was definitely not a high priority. For Him the most important thing—His Top Priority—was this:

> Seek first His [God's] kingdom, and His righteousness; and all these things shall be added to you (Matt. 6:33).

Because Jesus gave highest priority to seeking the Kingdom of God and His righteousness, we should be sure we know what He meant by these terms.

Where Is the Kingdom of God?

Scholars and theologians have written entire libraries about the Kingdom, but essentially it all boils down to one thing; the Kingdom of God is the place where God actively reigns; where His will is done.[3]

Many of the Jews of Jesus' day thought the Kingdom of God was a political one. They hated their Roman rulers, who had conquered Palestine in 64 B.C. When they talked about a Messiah, they meant a super human hero type who would crush the occupying Roman forces and then set up a glorious reign in Israel. Jesus, however, didn't have this plan in mind at all. He claimed to be the Messiah all right, but He planned to set up His Kingdom in the hearts of those who would believe in Him.

Jesus was talking about a spiritual kingdom, not an earthly one. He was looking for subjects who would willingly seek His Kingdom, enter it by faith and then obey Him as sovereign Lord. Even His disciples, especially Judas, really didn't understand this.

What Is "God's Righteousness"?

As for God's righteousness, there are two kinds. In one sense our Christian righteousness is our standing before God. God declares us righteous when we believe in Christ as Saviour (see Rom. 3:22-24; 2 Cor. 5:21).[4]

But in another sense, righteousness means purity of heart, doing what we know we should, being and doing right.[5] That's why Jesus said, "Blessed are those who hunger and thirst for righteousness, for they shall be satisfied" (Matt. 5:6).

To seek first the Kingdom of God and His righteousness means to try to live a holy life in accordance with God's will. Remember, however, we can't live a righteous life in our own strength and strictly on our own efforts. That would be *self*-righteousness. But as we trust in Christ as Saviour and Lord and seek to serve Him, we become righteous in practical, specific ways. Our lives will show it. That's what Paul meant when he wrote to the church at Philippi and told them they had been "filled with the fruits of righteousness" (Phil. 1:11).

To sum up, when Jesus tells us to seek first the Kingdom of God and His righteousness, He is not telling us how to become Christians; He is telling us how to live because we *are* Christians.[6] Our relationship to our heavenly Father is, without doubt, to be our top priority.

WHAT IS REALLY IMPORTANT
COMES FIRST, NOT SECOND.

28

CHAPTER 4

A PLAN FOR STRAIGHTENING OUT PRIORITIES

When we read Jesus' words about seeking first the Kingdom of God it all seems simple enough—or does it? Jesus may tell us to put God first, but *do* we? One way to find out is to examine what really takes priority in our lives.

Take a Look at Your Priorities

Try ranking the following four names in order of importance to *you*. Put a 1 by the most important, a 2 by the next most important and so on. Remember to be honest. Tell it like it is, not like you think it should be.

_____O.J. Simpson
_____Billy Graham
_____Anita Bryant
_____The apostle Paul

Here is another list, with four different activities. Rate them from 1 (first) to 4 (last) in priority, according to your present life-style.

———working—your job, career, etc.
———watching TV
———having Bible study
———spending time with friends

Try ranking one more list, from 1 (first) to 4 (last) to identify some of your most basic priorities.
Most important to me among the following are:

———getting plenty of exercise, recreation
———being good at what I do
———being kind and loving
———being popular or successful

How did that one come out? Note that there really aren't any bad choices in the list. All four are worthy things to be or do. But which one would be most Christian? Which one would come closest to "seeking God and His righteousness"? The Bible does not condemn skill, popularity, recreation or success. In fact, you can find mini-formulas for achieving most of these in the book of Proverbs.[1] But the Bible has a great deal more to say about being kind and loving.[2]

No matter how you "scored" on the above lists, be aware that priorities are tricky. And they vary, depending on the time and the situation. Nobody—and I mean nobody—puts God first 100 percent of the time. The only person who ever did was Jesus and He had an edge (see John 10:30).

What Can I Do About My Priorities?

So far we have discovered:

First, our priorities are a nitty-gritty picture of our

WHAT HAPPENS IF WE FAIL TO PUT GOD FIRST?

values. What we choose to do, use or enjoy first is what we really value (unless we have to put certain things first due to pressure, danger, etc.).

Second, Jesus clearly taught us to put the Kingdom of God and His righteousness first in our lives (see Matt. 6:25-33).

Third, nobody bats .1000 at putting God first. Other things, desires, needs, etc., keep slipping in higher on our priority lists.

So what should we do if we fail to always put God first? Turn in our citizenship papers for the Kingdom of God? That option doesn't look too appealing. We want to stay in God's Kingdom, but does that mean we go around feeling continually guilty because we don't always put Him first?

The answer is a simple no. God saves us in the first place, not because we are good enough, but because He loves and forgives us. And God continues to accept and forgive us, not because we live perfect lives, but because He is our loving Father. God knows where He is on each

31

of our priority lists, but—wonder of wonders—that doesn't put us any lower on His priority list!

Practical Steps toward Better Priorities

So, here is a basic plan of attack on this business of straightening out our priorities:

Start sorting out your priorities at every opportunity. What *does* come first in your life? Do your priorities ever change? If so, when? On a certain day of the week? At a certain time of year? With certain people? Why do they change?

Following is a list of 10 items that probably play a part in your life. Try ranking them from 1 to 10 in importance. Really *try*, even if you can't be absolutely sure about each choice. Tell it like it *is*, then decide on how you want it to become. What items do you want to raise higher? How do you intend to do it? What items need to be lowered? How will you do that?

_____physical appearance and condition

_____sports and recreation

_____education

_____earning or receiving money

_____being organized, orderly living

_____prayer, devotional life

_____church program, activities

_____family activities and needs

_____friends and social life

_____television, movies and entertainment

_____witnessing, sharing my faith with non-Christians as well as Christians

_____clothes, cars, the comfortable life

Stay in close touch with God through prayer to learn His priorities for your life. If you have put your faith in

Christ as Saviour and Lord, you are part of God's Kingdom—that place where He rules, where His will is to be done. As you are able to seek first His Kingdom and His righteousness, you will be amazed at its effect on how you arrange your priorities.

At first you may not make much progress. You may get hung up on worrying about the "basics"—having enough of what you think you need to get by in this crazy pressure cooker world. But never give up on straightening out your priorities, on moving God up the ladder to the very top. How can you lose? You have His own promise:

MAKE GOD'S KINGDOM AND HIS WAY OF DOING THINGS FIRST IN YOUR LIFE AND HE WILL GIVE YOU EVERYTHING YOU NEED.

CHAPTER 5

NOT TO DECIDE IS IMPOSSIBLE!

Decisions, decisions! We all face them. Some are small:

Eggs scrambled or sunny-side up? Wear the blue sweater or the gray? Go for a walk or take a nap?

Other decisions are more important:

Write checks to pay the monthly bills or watch TV? Stop for gas or try to make it to the other side of town? Lay the brown shade of carpet or the beige?

Some decisions are still bigger:

Put your daughter in the expensive Christian college or let her attend the local junior college? Take the chairmanship of the church board or have more time for your family? Accept the promotion and move across country or stay where you are with less salary but solid roots in a community your family really likes?

And then there are the world shakers:

Truman's decision to use the atomic bomb on Japan

to end World War II; Kennedy's decision to blockade Cuba in 1962; Nixon's decision to stonewall the Watergate investigation.

Do decisions have anything to do with values? Actually, *values have everything to do with decisions.* What we think or feel is important and worthwhile can affect our decisions practically every minute of the day. And how good or bad we are at making decisions has an awful lot to do with making our lives happy or unhappy, successful or frustrated, meaningful or just blah.

What Did Jesus Say About Decision Making?

Jesus spoke often about the far-reaching effect of decisions. For example, the man who decides to build his house upon the sand will see it fall, but the man who builds upon the rock will see it stand, no matter how strong the storms (see Matt. 7:24-27). Jesus gave the rich young ruler the choice between keeping his riches or selling all and following Him (Luke 18:18-24). In Matthew 6:24 He tells us we must choose; we cannot serve God and Mammon (money).

Jesus also faced decisions, and so did His disciples. One of the most dramatic decision-making episodes happened just after Jesus had performed one of His most spectacular miracles—feeding the 5,000 (John 6:1-12).

After Jesus feeds the huge crowd on the western shore of the Sea of Galilee, the people want to make Him their king. But He slips away with His disciples and turns up the next morning on the eastern side of the lake, at the synagogue in Capernaum. The crowd follows, their enthusiasm still running high. They see in Jesus the kind of leader they have been looking for. Here is a man with super powers. Not only is He a walking McDonald's, but surely He can free them from the hated rule of the Roman soldiers who occupy their land. Surely He can

35

lead Israel back to the glorious heights it has known in the past.

Jesus faces a decision: Go along with the crowd and let them crown Him "king" or set them straight. He decides to set them straight.

In a matter of seconds Jesus pops the crowd's balloon by telling them He has not come to be their meal ticket or political leader. He has come to give them bread all right, but a different kind of bread:

> *I am the bread of life; he who comes to Me shall not hunger, and he who believes in Me shall never thirst* (John 6:35).

The crowd doesn't understand. Isn't this fellow, Jesus, the son of Mary and Joseph? How can a common carpenter talk this way?

Jesus doesn't back off but goes on to say:

> *I am the living bread that came down out of heaven; if anyone eats this bread, he shall live forever; and the bread also which I shall give for the life of the world is My flesh* (John 6:51).

But the crowd remains puzzled. They can't understand that Jesus is talking about *spiritual* matters. They continue to think in physical terms and even speculate: "How can this man give us His flesh to eat?" (see John 6:52).

So, Jesus expands His startling ideas with even more emphasis:

> *Truly, truly, I say to you, unless you eat the flesh of the Son of Man and drink His blood, you have no life in yourselves. He who eats My flesh and drinks My blood has eternal life; and I will raise him up on the last day. For My flesh is true food, and My blood is true drink. He who eats My flesh and drinks My blood abides in Me, and I in him. As the living Fa-*

ther sent Me, and I live because of the Father;
so he who eats Me, he also shall live because
of Me (John 6:53-57).

The Crowd Decides to Call It Quits

At this point many in the crowd have pretty well had it. All of this "eat my flesh and drink my blood" talk is too much for them. They, too, make a decision. They will abandon Jesus and not follow Him anymore (see John 6:66).

It is a tense moment. The crowd is filing out of the synagogue. Word is already being passed in the streets: "Forget this fellow, Jesus. He is some kind of a nut, not the one we're looking for at all."

Still standing near Jesus, however, are his 12 disciples —Peter, James, John, Andrew and the others He handpicked to live with and learn from Him. How has His sudden plunge in popularity affected them? What will they decide? Jesus turns to His 12 friends and says, in effect: "What about you? Are you dumping me, too?" (see John 6:67).

It is the moment of decision for the 12 disciples. They know that the tide has turned against them. Jesus, the overnight superstar, has practically fallen off the charts. All they can expect from here on is second rate billing and sleazy accommodations. No more autograph hunters; no more oohs and ahhs when they walk in. Instead, just sneers, jibes, quizzical looks and suspicion. Their chance to make their mark in the world has gone down the drain with one speech. If only Jesus could have been a bit more diplomatic. If only He could have watered things down, gone a bit slower with this "bread of life" approach—

But suddenly Peter speaks up. Never known for being an intellectual giant, Peter nonetheless is no spiritual

37

pygmy. Some of what Jesus had been saying has soaked in. Peter doesn't always understand this fellow Jesus, but there is something about Him that rings true. So Peter makes his decision and says:

> *Lord, to whom shall we go? You have words of eternal life. And we have believed and have come to know that You are the Holy One of God* (John 6:68,69).

If anyone among the Twelve was wavering, Peter's dramatic statement must have bolstered him. Even Judas, the one who would betray Jesus, decides to stick around for awhile and see how things will come out.

Decisions Are Always with Us

Jesus and His disciples went on from that turning point at Capernaum to make many more decisions, some of which were even more difficult and complicated. Something we should always remember is that Jesus had to wrestle with decision-making just as we do. He was man as well as God. The writer of the letter to the Hebrews tells us that Jesus "did not come as an angel but as a human being . . . he himself has been through suffering and temptation" (Heb. 2:16,18, *TLB*).

Jesus wasn't some kind of spiritual bionic robot who moved through life with nary a qualm or quiver. He was flesh and blood. He felt things. He made choices. He also agonized over decisions, such as the one in the Garden of Gethsemane when the thought of being crucified almost made Him want to back out (see Matt. 26:36-46).

But Jesus didn't make decisions haphazardly. He didn't pluck the petals off daisies, nor did He play eeny-meeny-miney-mo. Jesus always based His decisions on His values. He knew what was important and what He had to do. He had His head together and knew how and why to make each decision that came His way.

It's easy, of course, to say, "Well, I'm not Jesus. Making decisions will always be hard for me." And that may be true. Decision making has always been a problem for some of us. Somehow we lack the gift of being able to decide quickly. Probably more important, we lack the ability to live with our decisions afterward without staring at the bedroom ceiling all night.

Fortunately, Jesus knew decisions could cause us problems. That is why He gave us His Holy Spirit to guide us, teach us and strengthen us.[1] No matter what we face, He is there to help. A well-known poster slogan tells us: "Not to decide is to decide."[2] If we cop out, put it off or say we "need more facts," it is still a decision. Not to decide is virtually impossible. The real issue is *how* we make our decisions:

WE CAN DECIDE WITH JESUS' HELP
OR WITHOUT IT.

CHAPTER 6

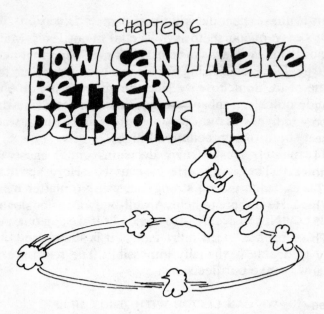

HOW CAN I MAKE BETTER DECISIONS?

What, exactly, is involved in making decisions? Why are some people able to make decisions almost immediately, while some of us never seem to make up our minds? Why do some people seem to always make good decisions (at least things come out right for them) while others are always doing something dumb?

How to Make Decisions—It's a Process

We base our decisions on what we know so we can get what we want. When facing a fairly important decision, here are some key questions to ask.[1]

1. *What exactly is the decision I must make?* (You can't really have a decision-making situation unless you have at least two choices. Clearly identify those choices.)

2. *What is important to me?* What do I want to do, achieve or reach? (Here's where your values come into

play. Different people will make different decisions, depending on what they think is important.)

3. *What do I know about this situation?* Where and how can I get more information if I need it? (Many times, *remembering* what you already know, and *thinking it through*, can save you all kinds of grief. A lot of poor decisions are made simply because people don't use the information available.)

4. *What are the risks or costs involved?* (Look at each choice available. What will happen if you choose option X? What about option Y? What do you *value* the most? What price are you willing to pay to reach your goal?)

5. *What is my plan for carrying out this decision?* (This is critical. A lot of people make decisions and then try to "work out the details later." Often, this approach leads to disaster.)

Jesus and the Decision-Making Process

Now that we have five steps for making good decisions, let's apply them to the incident at Capernaum, which we discussed in chapter 5, that cost Jesus His popularity but not His principles.

1. What was the decision Jesus faced? He could go along with the crowd and make them believe He would be a free meal ticket and maybe a super freedom fighter to boot, or He could tell them who He really was and what He had actually come to do (see John 6:1-25).

2. What were Jesus' values? Obviously, He placed far more importance on the spiritual condition of the people. He wanted them to be His committed disciples, not freeloaders following Him around having picnics.

3. What information did Jesus have and what did He need? He knew why the crowd had followed Him to Capernaum—to get more bread and to crown Him a political king. He knew His real goals—to save the lost.

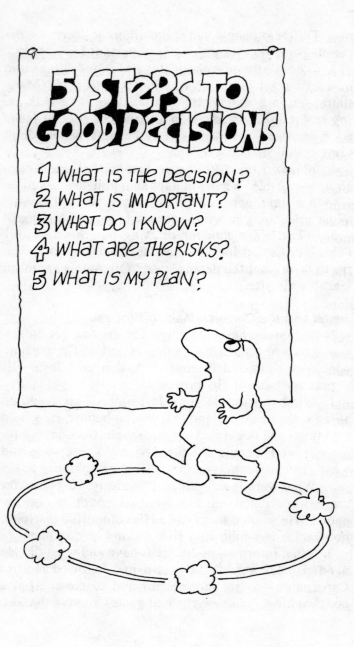

That was all the information He really needed.

4. What were the risks? If He went along with the crowd He would compromise His principles and purpose. If He told them the truth, He would lose His popularity.

5. What was Jesus' plan? Basically, He wanted to do the work He had been sent to do. After feeding the 5,000 to help convince them that He was God, He could see they had missed the point. So, He planned to set them straight at the right opportunity. The moment came the next day, at the synagogue in Capernaum. Jesus' decision cost Him popularity, but it gained far more.

The Crowd and the Decision-Making Process

Now let's look at the crowd and apply the five decision-making steps:

1. When Jesus told them who He really was and that free bread lines were not His style, the crowd could, (a) continue to follow Jesus or (b) drop Him like a hot barley loaf.

2. What values did the crowd hold? Apparently, material things—free bread, possibly being freed from the hated Romans—were most important to them.

3. What information did they have? They had seen or at least heard about the feeding of the 5,000. Some of them had possibly seen Jesus do other miracles. They knew this man had tremendous powers.

4. What were the risks or costs involved? If the crowd stayed with Jesus, it would mean a complete change of life-style. If they deserted Him, it meant turning their backs—at least temporarily—on His offer of eternal life (see John 6:60-65).

5. What was their plan? To not commit themselves to anything that meant sacrifice on their part. They always

had their escape hatch ready, and when Jesus asked for their commitment they decided to retreat in a hurry: "From that time many of his disciples ... walked no more with him" (John 6:66, *KJV*).

The Disciples and the Decision-Making Process

Finally, we have the Twelve, Jesus' handpicked companions and disciples.

1. Their decision was fairly simple: stay with Jesus, or desert with the rest of the crowd.

2. What were their values? A good question. Obviously, staying home and minding the store or the fishing nets did not appeal to them, or they would not have followed Jesus in the first place. On the other hand, they were normal human beings. Some of them, perhaps, may have been wondering if following Jesus any farther would really be worth the trouble.

3. They knew quite a bit about Jesus. They had heard Him teach, seen Him heal and perform other miracles. They knew He was no ordinary run-of-the-synagogue rabbi or prophet. They probably would have appreciated some additional explanations of what Jesus meant, but there wasn't any time for discussion. He had asked them if they had plans to leave too (see John 6:67).

4. The risks in sticking with Jesus now that His popularity had plunged were great. They would be despised, hooted, possibly even pelted by rocks or turned over to the Roman authorities as vagrants or revolutionaries. On the other hand, leaving Jesus meant cutting themselves off from the most intriguing, stimulating person they had ever met.

5. The disciples hardly had time to formulate a precise plan. Peter settled the issue for them. Perhaps Peter had planned to stick with Jesus all along and that is why, in so many words, he said, "Lord, where would we go?

You are the One we have been looking for. Nothing else matters." (See John 6:68,69.)

What Can I Do About My Decisions?

About now you might be thinking, "Applying the five decision-making steps to a Bible story is one thing, but I've got my own problems and decisions. As I look at my life things seem a *lot* more complicated."

In many respects life *is* more complicated today. Technology has "blessed" us to such an extent that we have far more things to do, people to see, and places to go than we can possibly cram into 24 hours a day or seven days a week. Life is, according to the old but still very accurate label, a rat race. Maybe that's why we need to use the five-step decision-making process every chance we get to use it. Granted, there are many decisions that must be made quickly, in a few seconds or a few minutes. Nobody expects you to run down the list of five steps if the house is on fire or if the traffic light just turned red. We make a lot of decisions each day that are automatic, or at least are apparently so simple that we don't need to use a step-by-step process in making them.

But what about the other kind of decisions—the ones where you do have two or more choices and there is some time to make up your mind? For practice, try applying the five-step decision-making process to these typical situations people face:

• Spend your Christmas bonus on: (a) new tires for the car (they could probably get by for another 1,000 miles); (b) a much needed vacation for the two of you—away from the kids; (c) a new dishwasher that will give everyone more free time.

• Attend a basketball tournament at the last minute with your father (who has spent quite a bit to get tickets)

45

or take your wife out to dinner as you have been promising to do for the last month.
• Use an unexpected inheritance check for $5,000 to: (a) start a college account for the children; (b) pay off several big credit card debts; (c) invest in some excellent income property.
• Tell your friends the truth about a certain couple you know or keep quiet and let them find out for themselves.

After applying the five-step decision-making process to the hypothetical situations suggested above, use it to make some real decisions you are facing right now. As you do so, here are some additional suggestions that can be of help.

First, add one more step to every decision—prayer. Jesus said, "Ask, and you will receive, that your joy may be made full" (John 16:24). First John 5:14 tells us "And this is the confidence which we have before Him, that, if we ask anything according to His will, He hears us."

Actually, prayer is something you can use when going through each of the five steps in the decision-making process.

Second, think about how much influence the peer group has on your decisions (circle one):
a great deal   quite a bit   some   very little

Third, think about how much influence Jesus has on your decisions (circle one):
a great deal   quite a bit   some   very little

Identifying just how much Jesus Christ really influences our daily decisions can be difficult. Some days are better than others. Some situations are easier than others.

We go to a Bible camp, a layman's conference, or an especially good church service and we get inspired, filled—practically "blessed out of our socks." And we make decisions: to accept Christ as Saviour, to rededicate our lives to Him, to read the Bible and pray more, to be nicer to our kids, our in-laws, the dog. But then we go back to the daily routine and the feeling seems to fade. We go from "I'll do what you want me to do, dear Lord," to "What in the world should I do now?"

All too often we forget the One who is supposed to be in charge of our lives. Instead, we think we can do our own thing, go our own way. Or worse, we don't think at all. Instead of making intelligent decisions, we just react, rely on instinct or intuition. Or, we just shuffle along with the crowd and let others make our decisions for us.

There is much we can learn from that scene in the synagogue at Capernaum. Peter, the big lovable loud-mouth fisherman, sometimes had a hard time getting things straight, but one thing he had very straight was just who should be at the center of his values. No matter how tightly the world tries to squeeze us into its mold, we can do no better than to say with Peter:

LORD, WHERE CAN WE TURN BUT TO YOU?
YOU OFFER ETERNAL LIFE
AND EVERYTHING ELSE WORTH HAVING.

HOW MUCH DO I VALUE GOD? PART II

7. What Is Jesus Worth to Me?
8. How Can I Feel Closer to Christ?

CHAPTER 7

WHAT IS JESUS WORTH TO ME?

As part of the research for this book, I surveyed several hundred people concerning their values. One of the questions I asked dealt with what they would like to do, be or have. That same question, containing a list of 26 choices, appears on the next page (fig. 1). (Just for fun, check off your own answers.)

When the survey results were in, items like "have a stronger faith in God" and "feel closer to Christ" were number one in practically all groups. What makes these results really interesting is that the people surveyed were all churchgoers, members of Sunday School classes, who had gone to church anywhere from several weeks to all their lives.

On the surface these statistics might look discouraging to all the pastors, youth workers and teachers involved with the people who were surveyed. After all their work many of those in their classes and congregations still needed to feel closer to Christ, to have a stronger faith in God.

Put a check by the statements that best describe you. I would like to:

_____a. have a more satisfactory life-style

_____b. not let the world squeeze me into its mold

_____c. make better decisions

_____d. have better relationships with my family

_____e. be able to control my temper better

_____f. be more popular

_____g. have a stronger faith in God, Christ

_____h. find more meaning in life

_____i. please myself for a change, rather than always give in to others

_____j. understand the Bible better

_____k. know more about how to handle my sexuality

_____l. learn not to waste so much of my time

_____m. know how to pick the right person to marry

_____n. live in a way that backs up what I say I believe

_____o. have more dates

_____p. have a job to earn spending money

_____q. be able to communicate better with my family

_____r. know more about what it takes to make a lasting, successful marriage

_____s. learn how to handle my feelings

_____t. feel closer to Christ

_____u. learn how to set goals and reach them

_____v. have a more effective prayer life

_____w. be a kinder, more loving person

_____x. learn more about who I really am

_____y. be sure my life will be worthwhile

_____z. be able to like myself better

Now go back over each statement you checked. Put an "X" by the top three.

Figure 1

On the other hand, maybe this survey reveals something that is true of almost all followers of Jesus Christ. We value Him—to some degree or other—but we are not sure just how much. What is He really "worth" to us? Some of us feel far away from Him and we would like to be a lot closer. Some of us feel very close, and would like to be even closer. And there are probably a lot of us who don't feel He is a million miles away but He doesn't exactly seem to be next door either.

Interestingly enough, Jesus' 12 disciples had these same feelings. They lived with Him for three years. They walked the dusty roads with Him. They heard Him teach. He held special "skull sessions" just for them to explain His parables. They watched Him do miracles. He saved them from a storm on the Sea of Galilee. But even on the night before He was to die on the cross, they still didn't quite know who He was. They had just been through a very personal experience with Him—the Last Supper—but their faith was still weak, their understanding a bit cloudy.

What Did Jesus Say About Himself?

Some of the most amazing things Jesus ever said about Himself are in the opening verses of John 14. The scene is the Upper Room where Jesus and His disciples observed the first communion service. They have eaten the bread (His body to be given for them) and they have drunk from the cup (His blood to be shed for their sins). He has washed their feet to show them what real love for one another is all about. And now He says:

"Let not your heart be troubled; believe in God, believe also in Me. In My Father's house are many dwelling places; if it were not so, I would have told you; for I go to prepare a place for you. And if I go and prepare a place for

you, I will come again, and receive you to
Myself; that where I am, there you may be
also. And you know the way where I am go-
ing."

Thomas said to Him, "Lord, we do not
know where You are going; how do we know
the way?"

Jesus said to him, "I am the way, and the
truth, and the life; no one comes to the Father,
but through Me" (John 14:1-6).

To see why Jesus begins chapter 14 by saying, "Let
not your heart be troubled," you have to go back to the
end of chapter 13. He has just told the devoted, but
overconfident, Peter that before the cock crows he will
deny his Lord three times. This pronouncement had to
be disappointing for the disciples. Peter was their
spokesman, a natural leader. If *he* was going to fail, what
about *them?*[1]

Jesus senses their dismay and tells them not to worry.
They believe in God, they can believe in Him. He is
making reservations for them at His Father's house and
someday they will live with Him there. Furthermore,
they know the way to where He is going.

About this time, Thomas is muttering something like,
"Wait a minute, what is Jesus talking about?" Jesus is
thinking of heaven, of course, but Thomas is not on His
wavelength. He tells Jesus that he and the other disciples don't even have an address for the Father's house
so how can they know the way?

Jesus' reply makes Him one of two things. Anyone
who would say, "I am the way, and the truth and the life;
no one comes to the Father but through Me," is either
someone very special, or a candidate for the cuckoo's
nest.

When Jesus said, "I am the way," He didn't mean that

He was going to turn into a road or a footpath. He meant something else, something every Christian should thank God for daily. It is one thing to just tell someone the way. For example all of us know what it's like to ask directions in a strange town or city:

"The expressway heading west? Well, you have to go down here about three blocks—no, it's four lights—at the fourth light—or is it the fifth? Never mind, you'll see this gas station on the corner. Turn left and go six more lights, then turn right, go over the underpass and double back to the stop sign. Turn right and it's three blocks to the expressway onramp, unless it's still closed for repairs, then you'll have to—"

When it comes to getting to the Father's house, Jesus doesn't just tell us the way by reeling off some confusing directions. Instead He says, "Come, I'll take you to the Father's house myself. I'll walk with you. I'll lead you. I'll give you strength and guide you personally."[2]

Jesus wasn't just another teacher telling people about a way they could get to God. He made the flat-out claim that He was *the* Way—the *only* Way.

Thomas and the rest must have looked like a choir trying to hit a high note after hearing that one. But Jesus ignores their gaping mouths and goes on to say something even more staggering:

"If you had known Me, you would have known My Father also; from now on you know Him, and have seen Him."

Philip said to Him, "Lord, show us the Father, and it is enough for us."

Jesus said to him, "Have I been so long with you, and yet you have not come to know Me, Philip? He who has seen Me has seen the Father" (John 14:7).

Jesus often spoke in parables that were hard to understand, but this time He comes right out with it and says, in effect, "You want to see God? You are looking right at Him!" *That* remark had to be even more startling than His claim to be the way, the truth and the life. Something that has always bothered people since the dawn of history is that God seems so far away. God is so awesome, so terrible, so austere and frightening. He is a ruler who is seemingly too important to bother with us, to get His hands dirty in our mundane affairs. But in Jesus Christ God came close. He entered human history. He invaded our planet. He became flesh and blood and lived among us. He dirtied His hands in more ways than one to bring us His love.

Silent Night, Incredible Night

We all know the Christmas story. Every year we celebrate it; we sentimentalize it; we commercialize it. What we *should* do every December is call for two or three weeks of silence while we stand in awe of what God did on that silent night so long ago.

In Jesus, God became part of an ordinary family. He even took the trouble and pain to be born just like the rest of us. He didn't suddenly appear full grown in royal robes. He had to learn to eat, to endure wet diapers, to learn not to cut His fingers on Joseph's carpenter tools. As one poet put it:

> *Little Jesus, wast Thou shy*
> *Once, and just so small as I?*
> *And what did it feel to be*
> *Out of Heaven and just like me?*[3]

In Jesus, God loved us. In fact, He loved us so much He went to the cross. It is hard to picture a "king" who would willingly do this. Kings, emperors, dictators, and others with absolute power have not been known for their self-sacrifice. In fact, they have usually been known for the opposite, especially if any of their subjects stepped out of line.

In ancient times, if the king didn't like you it could mean anything from having your eyes put out to being skinned alive or boiled in oil. During the twentieth century we have seen the work of Lenin and Stalin, communist dictators who sent millions to slavery or death in Siberia.[4] Hitler's Holocaust—a maniacal attempt to exterminate the Jewish race during World War II—is forever burned into our memories.

In recent years Idi Amin, ruler of the African nation of Uganda, has murdered over 300,000 of his subjects. Bodies piled up so high they had to be buried in mass graves or tossed to the crocodiles in the Nile River. On February 18, 1977 Amin ordered hundreds of the Langi tribe (who are mostly Christians) to be clubbed or strangled to death because he thought they were plotting against him.[5]

But in Jesus we see a King who did not persecute and murder. By His own choice *He* was persecuted and murdered by those in rebellion against Him and His heavenly Father. Why? To take care of our major problem—sin. In Jesus, God Himself died for our sins, because He loved us. And He loves us still. He never gets tired of us, never gets fed up with us, always cares, always understands, always forgives when we sincerely repent and ask forgiveness.

Jesus' *value* is incalculable. What He is *worth* to us depends on how carefully we listen to His words:

HE IS THE WAY, THE TRUTH AND THE LIFE.
THERE IS NO OTHER.

CHAPTER 8

HOW CAN I FEEL CLOSER TO CHRIST?

In passages like John 14 and many other places,[1] the Bible makes it clear that God lived among us. Through Jesus we can know God *personally*.

Knowing that we can become personally acquainted with God through Jesus Christ is exciting, but it doesn't necessarily solve the problem of feeling closer to Him. We know God puts high value on us. He sent His only Son to give us eternal life. But how much effect does this have on our lives? We *know* God is close, but do we *feel* that way?

Take a Look at Your Picture of Jesus

One way to find out is to take a look at just how well we know this man they called Jesus. The one who never lost His cool, never got rattled. The one who said and did wonderful things. The one who finally died on a cross and was buried in a tomb behind a gigantic stone. The one who rose from the dead and talked again with His disciples.

For example, how do you think Jesus looked? When you picture Him in your mind's eye, what do you see? (Underline one):

soft white skin/leathery suntan
sinew and muscle/not much of a build
a loud resonant voice/a soft but clear voice
quick energetic movements/steady, unhurried pace

(It may be difficult to come up with a very clear idea of how Jesus looked and acted, but try putting down your ideas. For centuries a vicious rumor has circulated which labels Jesus as soft and effeminate. Did the first image that came to your mind give you that kind of picture, or something else?)

Now try describing Jesus as a person. Which of the following seem to fit Him best? (Underline one):

a dynamic orator/a quiet confident teacher
a powerful leader/a gentle counselor
someone you can talk to/someone you better listen to

(Granted, choosing between some of these combinations may be difficult because sometimes both seem to fit. But try to pick the descriptions that seem most applicable, as far as you are concerned. It will help you get a sharper picture of just *who* Jesus is to *you*.)

Next, try to picture what your relationship to Jesus is really like. Pick the phrase that is most accurate for you, right now (underline one):

Walking with Christ is like:
going uphill
climbing a mountain
going downhill
uphill and downhill

Spending time with Jesus is like:
a ride in a camper van
a ride in the family sedan
a ride in a sports car
a ride on a motorcycle

Trying to communicate with Jesus is like:
talking to the wall
chatting with a good friend
an interview with your boss
listening to your pastor
talking with an understanding counselor

Making choices like those above may be fun or frustrating. Everyone is different, with different perceptions and ideas. Maybe very few of the choices fit your own ideas of who Jesus is to you. But the thing to do is use these suggestions as starters to paint your own picture of who Jesus is to you. It may give you some clues about why you feel far from Him, close to Him, or just sort of "in the neighborhood."

What Can I Do About Feeling Closer to Christ?

For most of us the problem is *not* a need to "get away from Jesus for awhile." According to the survey I conducted, about 90 percent of those polled wanted to move *closer* to Christ. When I asked them why, Mark, a candid young fellow, said, "It's hard to know someone you can't see."

HOW DO YOU HaVe a ReaL ReLaTIONSHIP WITH aN INVISIBLe, UNHUGGaBLe BeING?

His companion, Tim, added, "Because you can't see God, it's hard to develop a love for Him and feel close to Him. It's like having a good friend who moves away and you don't think of that friend as often. You begin thinking about yourself and other things. But if you correspond, you think about each other more. It's the same way with being a Christian. If you pray and read the Bible, you will be thinking more about Him and learn to love Him."

A career woman in her mid-twenties had this to say about God's invisible qualities: "We seem to be talking about how to have a tangible, real relationship with an invisible, untouchable, unsqueezable, unhuggable being. Once you've started that, how do you keep it going? The mind seems to forget that which isn't right in front of it all the time. Another part of the problem is that with real persons you talk to them, you see them smile—there is a response that translates into body language. Part of why we don't feel closer to Christ is the absence of this immediate feedback. So, we always go around feeling like 'I really ought to be doing better than I am.' "

Many of us would agree—we really ought to be doing better. But how? What specific and possible steps can we take to "feel closer to Christ," to "have a stronger faith in God"?

Thousands of books, magazines, pamphlets and tracts have been written to describe how it's done. Another several million sermons and devotionals have been given along the same line. Basically, they all zero in on three basic areas: the mental/spiritual; the social/spiritual; the emotional/spiritual.

The Quiet Time Connection

The mental/spiritual area has always been a problem for most, if not all, Christians. Whatever we want to call it—devotions, quiet time, Bible reading and prayer—few of us seem to pull it off consistently. We all know what it's like to vow (again) to read the Bible through in a year or to spend at least 10 minutes a day in prayer. We have great intentions, but usually they don't materialize.

If our salvation really depended on how faithfully we read God's Word and talked to Him, hell would be crowded indeed. Fortunately, our salvation depends on God's grace with no strings (works on our part) attached. However, our growth (sanctification) as Christians does depend in great measure on how much input we get from God's Word. The Bible is the only real resource we have for knowing who God is, what He has done and how He wants us to live. As Jesus said, we don't live by bread alone. We need the words that come from the mouth of God (see Matt. 4:4).

There is no easy answer, but Tim's idea about keeping in touch with a friend by letter is a good one. As he says, you have to develop a discipline to hang on to (or gain) feelings of closeness to Christ. It all comes back to this business of values. If feeling closer to Christ is really important to you, reading God's Word has to be important also. Check the following suggestions for Bible reading and prayer. Which one seems to fit you best at the moment?

For me, the most realistic approach to a quiet time (Bible reading and prayer) is:
_____a few minutes once a week
_____5-10 minutes at least twice a week
_____10-15 minutes 3 or 4 times a week
_____daily quiet time, anywhere from a few minutes to half an hour

After picking a plan that seems to fit you, try it for a month or two. Keep a record of how well you do. Don't get discouraged if you miss now and then or have a completely zero week. Just acknowledging this to the Lord is a way to draw closer to Him. He's not asking for perfection, just your honest desire for fellowship.

The Body Life Connection

A popular term among many Christians in recent years is "body life"—meaning the fellowship believers can have with each other. In 1 Corinthians 12, the apostle Paul talks about how all those who believe are baptized into one Body of Christ, which should function together. Being together with other Christians that you enjoy and trust is a vital way to feel closer to Christ.

As Jesus said, "Where our treasure is, there will our hearts be also" (see Matt. 6:21). We do what we feel is valuable and worthwhile. Take a quick inventory on your own body life connection. Is it strong, in need of Geritol, or nonexistent?

For me, meaningful interaction with other Christians means:

_____church worship service

_____attending Sunday School

_____talking with one or two good Christian friends

_____meeting regularly with a group that really cares about one another

Keep in mind that your social/spiritual needs can be much different than someone else's. Some of us like to talk and share, to open up and let it all hang out. Others are more quiet, more "inside themselves." What is important, however, is that you have some kind of Christian support system—a place, a time, a group where you feel part of something that is bigger than you are, where you draw strength from others.

The "Brother Lawrence" Connection

Perhaps the best way to feel closer to Christ is to consciously include Him in your activities through the day. Easily said, not so easily done. One way to meet your emotional/spiritual needs is to make prayer a lot more spontaneous. You need quiet times for meditation on God's Word and talking with Him, but there is no law in the Bible that says you can't send up a quick word any time of the day or night, depending on the situation. Scripture teaches us to "Pray without ceasing" (1 Thess. 5:17), and you can literally do this as you make an important phone call, do the laundry or arrive late to work, just as the boss walks out of his office.

The possibilities are unlimited, but the hindrances seem to be unlimited also. It is far more natural to think about the world around you than to think about Christ. As one young fellow I talked to put it during one of our values discussions, "Lots of times you forget about Christ because you get wrapped up in other things."

A key point to always remember is that Satan will do everything he can to keep us away from Christ. In its ultimate sense, that is what hell is all about—being separated from Christ. If we get our minds on our problems, our schedules, our plans and, above all, just on ourselves, we will forget that Jesus is as close as a quickly whispered, "Help, Lord, what do I do about *this*?"

A little book that every Christian should read several times a year is *The Practice of the Presence of God*. It was written by Nicholas Herman, who became a lay brother in a Carmelite monastery near Paris, France in 1666 and was afterwards known as "Brother Lawrence." What can such an old book have to do with feeling closer to Christ in the future-shocked twentieth century?

Everything.

Poor, uneducated, and big and clumsy to boot, Brother Lawrence spent 25 years in the monastery, where he worked mostly in the hospital kitchen. He spent endless hours peeling vegetables, scrubbing pots and pans, and doing other grubby jobs that most of us don't associate with "Ten Easy Steps to Spiritual Victory." Yet Brother Lawrence was still known throughout the monastery and far beyond for his quiet, smiling serene faith in Christ. No matter how hectic things got in that hospital kitchen (and hospital kitchens were just as busy in the 1600s as they are today), Brother Lawrence was always calm, congenial, happy and helpful.

His secret? He simply practiced the presence of God.

His "formula"? In *The Practice of the Presence of God*, you will find not a formula, but a gold mine of practical, simple ideas.

Brother Lawrence established a sense of God's presence by continually talking with Him.[2]

He confessed his failures to God, but never dwelled

on them. Instead he would pray for God's forgiveness and correction, which in contemporary terms might have sounded something like this:

Lord, I'll continue to foul things up if you let me. You have to keep me from falling. You have to put my broken pieces back together.[3]

He set times for private devotions but put more emphasis on developing what he called the "actual presence" of God. He made a decision to never willfully forget God and to spend his entire life in God's presence, no matter what the situation.[4]

Brother Lawrence believed that everyone is capable of practicing the presence of God ("some more, some less. He knows what we can do").[5]

He was far from perfect. For example, he knew what it was like to have his mind wander while he was praying. His remedy was simple: confess the problem, ask the Lord's forgiveness and *be brief*. Brother Lawrence was a firm believer in short prayers (the long ones only cause your mind to start wandering again!).[6]

Do Brother Lawrence's ideas sound hard to understand? No, but they may sound difficult. He bores right into the heart of the whole question of feeling closer to Christ. If you want to feel close to Christ then you have to really *want to move* closer to Christ.

There is an old saying that goes something like this: "If God seems far away, guess who moved." According to Brother Lawrence, the more we move toward God, the closer we will feel. How do you move toward God? A few days before he died at the age of 80, Brother Lawrence wrote:

Let us seek Him often by faith. He is within us: seek Him not elsewhere . . . Let us begin to be devoted to Him in good earnest. Let us cast everything besides out of our hearts.[7]

It is almost as if Brother Lawrence was picturing that scene following the Last Supper when Philip said to Jesus, "Show us the Father, and it is enough for us" (John 14:8). Philip wanted to see God, but what Philip didn't realize was that God was standing right in front of him. It is the same with us. We want to feel closer to Christ, and He is *already* close. He is within us. If that is worth anything, it is worth remembering daily as we practice the presence of God Himself.

HE WHO TRUSTS CHRIST TRUSTS THE FATHER
AND THE FATHER WORKS IN HIM.

HOW MUCH DO I VALUE MYSELF?

PART III

9. He's Okay—I'm Okay
10. You Are More Than a Square Root, Charlie Brown!
11. How Can I Feel Good About Me?

CHAPTER 9

HE'S OK ooo I'M OK

What is the most important thing in life for most people? What is the basic driving force that motivates us, worries us, exhilarates us, or depresses us?

Perhaps it all depends on where you are in life's journey. In his book, *Is There Life After High School?*, Ralph Keyes makes a strong case for the idea that when you're in high school the thing that really matters is *status*.

To research his book Keyes interviewed hundreds of adults and asked them about their most vivid memories of high school. He was intrigued by the answers. Two things that people seemed to remember with uncommon accuracy were how many times their picture was in the school yearbook and the caption beneath their senior picture.[1]

The word Keyes heard more than any other as he quizzed people about their high school experiences was "embarrassed." Like the 45-year-old ex-jock who was embarrassed because he got only two letters his senior year instead of three. What embarrassed him most, however, was that he was still remembering it, and talking about it.[2]

Keyes believes that the reason people can recall *now* what mattered most *then* (in high school) is that they were concerned about that mystical quality called "status." He devised a quiz to show the difference between status and non-status. On the status side the answers included things like:
• arriving late to class, but always able to drop just the right quip to make everyone—including the teacher—laugh;
• breaking your leg while skiing and having everyone autograph your cast;
• showing up late at the important parties;
• having lots of people honk and wave when you cruise the drive-in on Saturday night.

On the non-status side the answers included:
• showing up at the favorite hamburger spot on Saturday night with your parents;
• having to ask the janitor to open your locker (between classes) because you forgot the combination;
• making Honor Society in your junior year;
• consistently arriving for class early.

You may or may not agree with all of author Keyes' opinions on what brings status in high school.[3] The point is, the desire for status is a powerful drive that reaches a high pitch in high school and often continues throughout life. Even adults in their forties, fifties and beyond can still remember what it was like to have, or lack, status back there in high school.

Just what is behind this drive for status? Dr. Robert Schuller, pastor of Garden Grove Community Church, Anaheim, California suggests that what all of us want more than anything else in this world is to feel that *we*

69

are worth something. He claims that all other drives, such as survival, pleasure or power, are only outward expressions of this need for status and self-worth—feeling good about who and what we are. What we all want, says Dr. Schuller, is *dignity.* We want to be able to know and appreciate ourselves.[4] In other words, we need self-love.

What Did Jesus Say About Self-Love?

Probably the best known description Jesus gave us concerning self-love is contained in His answer to the scribe who wanted to know, "What is the greatest commandment of all?"

Jesus answered in two parts. First, love the Lord your God with all your heart, soul, mind and strength. Second, love your neighbor *as you love yourself* (see Mark 12:28-31). There are two ways the Bible scholars look at what Jesus said about loving your neighbor as yourself. Some say the primary meaning is to be unselfish, to do for your neighbor what you would do for yourself (a la the Golden Rule).[5]

But a possible secondary meaning might be this: If first we love God, that will make us more capable of loving ourselves. And if we love ourselves, then we will be able to love our neighbor as we should. If someone fails to love his neighbor as himself, he is displaying pride or selfishness that is characteristic of someone who does not have healthy self-love or self-esteem.

Healthy self-esteem produces the kind of Christian living that results in loving your neighbor as much as yourself. Poor self-esteem produces just the opposite.

Healthy self-esteem has nothing to do with being proud, arrogant, or conceited. To have healthy self-esteem is to feel good about yourself in a realistic yet positive way. You realize you aren't perfect. You do not

HeALTHY SELF-ESTeeM MeaNS FeeLING GOOD ABOUT YOURSELF IN a ReaLISTIC YeT POSITIVe waY

GOD DON'T Make NO JUNK

consider yourself better than others. Instead you are thankful to God for how He made you (big ears, long nose and all). You don't waste time wishing you were tall and willowy rather than short and a bit on the chunky side. You don't argue with God about why He seemed to make so many beautiful and talented people, while He made you rather plain and average. You agree with the well-known poster that says: "God don't make no junk!"

God's Love Makes You Somebody

Self-esteem sounds like a great thing to have, so how do we get it—preferably in large doses every day? According to the teaching of Jesus Christ, the source of healthy self-esteem is God Himself. That's why His first great commandment was, "Love God with all your heart, soul, mind and strength." The reason we can reach out in love to God is that we know He first loved us (1 John 4:19).

Jesus talked a great deal about God's love and care. In Matthew 10 He gives His 12 disciples instructions before they go out on a preaching mission. He says they don't have to be afraid because:

*Are not two sparrows sold for a cent? And
yet not one of them will fall to the ground
apart from your Father. But the very hairs of
your head are all numbered. Therefore do not
fear; you are of more value than many sparrows* (Matt. 10:29-31).

Jesus is saying something very simple, but very important. God cares about the sparrows. He knows about
every one that falls to the ground injured or dead. In fact
one interpretation claims that God knows and cares
every time a sparrow even lights on the ground in search
of food.[6]

If God knows and cares about the sparrows, surely He
cares about us. According to Jesus' own words, we are
worth more to Him than many sparrows.

God Reads the Lost and Found Column

Jesus also spoke of God's love and care for all men
and women when He told the parable of the Prodigal
Son (see Luke 15:11-32). Since early Sunday School
days we have heard of the younger of two sons who
demanded his inheritance (even though his father was
still alive).

The younger son left home, went through the cash in
a hurry, and soon found himself feeding pigs. Realizing
he was in desperate shape, he decided to go back home
even if it meant punishment, the cold shoulder or a big
round of I-told-you-so's. Instead, when he got there, his
father trotted out the best calf in the herd, had it butch-
ered and barbecued, and threw a big party in his son's
honor.

The older son, who had stayed home and kept his
nose clean, got jealous and wanted to know why he had
served faithfully for all those years but had never been
given a party. The father simply said, "Look, you've

always been right here with me and everything I have is yours, but your brother I had given up as lost. Now he's back. He's found!"

Some Bible scholars believe the Parable of the Prodigal Son would be better named the Parable of the Loving Father. Not only does it teach that God loves you but that He forgives you as well. When you realize how much God loves you, you can only respond to Him with love in return. *God's love makes you somebody.* He is the very foundation of your self-esteem.

YOU AREN'T JUST WORTH "SOMETHING"—
YOU ARE WORTH EVERYTHING BECAUSE
GOD GAVE HIS ONLY SON FOR YOU.

CHAPTER 10

YOU ARE MORE THAN A SQUARE ROOT, CHARLIE BROWN!

To know that God is the foundation of our self-esteem is tremendously helpful. God is the all-powerful resource to whom we can turn to build a sound superstructure of good feelings about ourselves. But what we can't forget is that a literal army of saboteurs is ready to wreck our self-esteem, from the cradle through adulthood.

In his book, *Hide or Seek*, Dr. James Dobson describes graphically how all of us learn at an early age that as far as society is concerned the beautiful, talented and intelligent are the ones who are "worth" the most. Even five-year-olds can feel a lack of worth in our kind of system, which places value on people because they qualify or perform, not simply because they are persons made in God's image.

Dr. Dobson claims that an epidemic of inferiority infects society, particularly when we are between the ages of 12 and 20. Our school system, recognized as one of the best in the world, produces feelings of doubt and inadequacy in children from the early grades on. The ones who are cute, pretty, bright, well- coordinated, etc., make it. Despite possible reassurances by well-meaning teachers, coaches and advisors, many of the rest decide they are "losers."[1]

As Charlie Brown tells Lucy: "I hate being a nothing! I refuse to go through the rest of my life as a zero!"

"What would you like to be, Charlie Brown?" asks Lucy. "A five? Or a par seventy-two?"

And then Lucy has the answer: "I know what you could be, Charlie Brown . . . a square root! I think you'd make a great square root, Charlie Brown."

Charlie sums it up for us who don't like being zeros, square roots or minus tens: "I can't stand it!"[2]

Take a Look at Your Self-Esteem

Where are you on the self-esteem scale right now? How much or how well do you value yourself? How well do you know yourself? The better you know yourself the more easily you can identify your good qualities and also set goals to work on your weak spots.

Following are three brief quizzes containing three questions each. In each question you mark yourself on a scale of 1 to 10. Whatever number you mark is also your "score" for that question. The three quizzes are designed to help you evaluate your self-esteem and God, your self-esteem and your personality, your self-esteem and your talents and abilities.

My Self-Esteem and God

1	2	3	4	5	6	7	8	9	10

I'm not sure God values me very much. I goof a lot.

I'm always sure God values me a great deal, even when I goof.

75

1	2	3	4	5	6	7	8	9	10

I have many   I'm usually
doubts and   very sure of
I'm sure God   what I believe
is not happy   and I know God
with me   understands,
for this.   even when I
It's a sin   have doubts.
to doubt.

1	2	3	4	5	6	7	8	9	10

God makes a   God forgives
lot of demands   and accepts me,
and I don't always   even though I may
measure up.   fail to measure up
                                 to His standards.

Now total up your scores. If you scored 10 or lower for all three questions, the very foundation of your self-esteem—accepting God's love—is very shaky. You need to look for ways to strengthen your relationship to Him. It is imperative for you to remember that your self-esteem is based on what God—not someone else—thinks of you. If we think God is judging us on the basis of our performance only, we will respond to Him with guilt, shame and fear.

When our performance is weak or poor, which often happens, we will be unsure of our relationship to God and our self-esteem has to suffer. Performance-oriented Christians live in a cage labeled, "God won't really accept me if I fail."[3] God accepts us because of what Jesus Christ did for us on the cross, not because of our performance.

For just a few of the many places the Bible talks about how God accepts us through the cross, see Ephesians

1:5-7; Romans 3:24-28; Galatians 3:10-13; 1 Peter 1:18-21; and Ephesians 2:8-10. If possible, read these passages in a modern translation such as *Phillips.*

If your score totals 11-20, your relationship to God may be fairly solid, or it's possible you are living in that gray neutral zone, not feeling really good or bad about God's acceptance and forgiveness. Read the verses listed above and then try writing a prayer of thanksgiving for what they mean to you.

If you scored a total of 21-30, the indications are that you and God are on very good terms. If you still tend to slip back toward feeling that you must perform to win God's favor, have the verses listed above marked in a special way in your Bible and read them often. Keep in mind that God's forgiveness and acceptance of us through Christ does not mean we should ignore His guidelines for right living. We aren't saved *by* works but we are saved *to* work, out of love and gratitude, not fear and guilt.

Now that you have looked at your self-esteem and God, try thinking about your self-esteem and your personality.

My Self-Esteem and My Personality

1	2	3	4	5	6	7	8	9	10

I never get
involved,
people don't want
me anyway.

I always get
in on things,
people welcome me
to their group.

1	2	3	4	5	6	7	8	9	10

I keep
everything inside,
don't trust
other people much.

I let
everything out,
have no trouble
trusting others.

1	2	3	4	5	6	7	8	9	10

I am a loner, few friends, really don't like people much.

I am a mixer, have lots of friends, like people a lot.

If your total score for all three questions is 10 or less, it sounds like you are shy, passive, and don't communicate well with others. You may be on the introvert side, which means your thoughts and interests are turned inward. These characteristics can, and often do, undermine your self-esteem, because you are likely to think no one cares about you or needs you. We all need to feel that we can trust someone—family, brothers and sisters in Christ—and that they like us and respect us.

If your total score is 11-20, you are probably more typical, translated to show you as neither a strong introvert nor an all-out extrovert (which means your thoughts and interests are turned outward toward other people or things). You have a better chance of having excellent self-esteem. However, you need to bear in mind that a lot depends on the quality of your relationships with others, also. Living at a surface level (never really getting to know people nor being interested in investigating their real needs) will not build healthy self-esteem in anyone.

If your total score is 21-30, you are definitely on the extrovert side. Ironically, this doesn't automatically guarantee high self-esteem, as many extroverts can tell you. In fact, their initiative and aggressiveness are often a cover-up for a poor self-image. Again, the quality of your relationships and your real concern and interest for others are what help build solid self-esteem.

Another key self-esteem area is your abilities. What can you do and how well can you do it?

My Self-Esteem and My Talents, Abilities

| 1 | 2 | 3 | 4 | 5 | 6 | 7 | 8 | 9 | 10 |

I am
very lazy,
have no
ambition.

I am very
energetic,
have lots
of ambition.

| 1 | 2 | 3 | 4 | 5 | 6 | 7 | 8 | 9 | 10 |

I have no
talent or
ability, I'm
just sort of blah.

I have lots
of talents
and ability,
what I don't know,
I can learn.

| 1 | 2 | 3 | 4 | 5 | 6 | 7 | 8 | 9 | 10 |

I always fail,
I'm a total loser.

I almost
always succeed,
I'm a winner!

If your total score is 10 or lower, your self-esteem may almost be in shambles. Are you *sure* you are *that* lazy, *that* untalented, *always* a loser? Or is this just a lot of garbage certain people have been feeding you?

If your total score is 11-20 you're in that well-known average range. Your self-esteem is alive and in fairly good health, but it probably could be stronger. Are you sure you scored yourself high enough or are you trying to be "humble"?

If your total score is 21-30, you have a very good opinion of your talents and abilities, which is normally a strong builder of self-esteem. Even if you're not quite that good, the important thing is to honestly feel you are. We all live up to what is expected of us, by others or by ourselves.

Just for fun, add up your score for all three quizzes (all

nine questions). If you got 30 or less, it suggests you don't feel too good about yourself. A score of 31-60 says you feel fairly good about yourself, but probably not on a consistent basis. A score of 61-90 says you usually feel very good about yourself. (If you got 90, don't tell anyone; they might come after you with the butterfly net.)

One thing to keep in mind is that quizzes like these are not precise instruments for measuring self-esteem. No quiz or test will tell you the whole story. But what you can get from those nine questions are some indicators of your relationship to God, others and yourself. And if you don't feel too good about the results, you can start thinking about ways to improve the situation. (See chapter 11 for some practical ideas.)

There is no point in going through life feeling like a zero or a square root. You can feel like a par 72, a perfect 300 or a 5 million plus, as long as you keep self-love in proper perspective. If self-love goes to seed it turns inward and becomes sin. Biblical scholar John Stott points out that a mark of the last days is that men will be "lovers of self . . . rather than lovers of God" (see 2 Tim. 3:2,4). Stott feels that the term self-love can be misunderstood and misused until it becomes narcissism, autoeroticism or idolatry. He believes a better term than self-love is "self-acceptance."[4]

To sum up, there is the warped, selfish kind of self-love that separates you from God; and there is healthy, biblical self-love that enables you to accept yourself because you know God has accepted you, sins and all. Martin Luther put it well:

GOD DOES NOT LOVE US BECAUSE WE ARE VALUABLE.
WE ARE VALUABLE BECAUSE GOD LOVES US.

CHaPTeR 11

HOW CAN I FeeL GOOD ABOUT Me?

Healthy self-esteem is like any other form of good health. To have it, you need plenty of good nutrition and the right exercise. What you feed yourself (or allow others to feed you) is crucial. Daily workouts are also important.

In the area of self-esteem you feed yourself not food but *ideas*. If they are good, healthy ideas, your self-esteem will improve and even thrive. Feed yourself bad ideas, however, and your self-esteem will shrivel, wither and possibly die.

There are many books, seminars and courses on the market, all designed to help people gain better self-esteem. One of the best books I have found is by Dr. Ken Olson, who trained to be a clergyman and then shifted to a ministry in psychological counseling. Dr. Olson's book, which ties in nicely with biblical principles, is built on the premise that we should turn off our "negative tape recordings."

Where Do Those Negative Tapes Come From?

In *The Art of Hanging Loose in an Uptight World*, Dr. Olson claims that a major reason a lot of people are uptight, worried and lacking in self-esteem is because of the negative tapes they keep playing over and over in their heads. In other words they keep thinking negative ideas or keep telling themselves destructive things. All this is played over and over in their minds, just like a tape recording.

Dr. Olson discovered his negative tape concept while doing part-time sales work to finance his education. While attending seminary in Minneapolis, Minnesota, Olson decided to sell Watkins products door to door to add to his wife's earnings as a secretary. So, with a kit of vanilla, cinnamon, spices, liniment, cologne, etc., in hand he started knocking on doors.

He soon discovered that door-to-door salesmen often get far less than a warm welcome. He was called names, accused of being a nuisance (or worse) and often had the door slammed in his face. After a few days of this, Olson remembered a biblical passage he had been studying at seminary. When Jesus sent out His disciples to preach the gospel in nearby towns He told them they would face opposition. If a home did not receive them, they were to shake the dust from their feet and go on to the next one (see Mark 6:7-12). Salesman Olson decided to see if this idea of "shaking off the dust" could work in his own situation. He vowed he would shake off the bad memory of rejections by cranky housewives and go right on to the next house. The strategy did work and he became a successful seller of Watkins products. Instead of finding more and more surly and cranky people, he

WHAT IF I BLOW IT? WHY TRY? I CAN'T...

WE ALL PLAY OUR OWN KIND OF NEGATIVE TAPES

found more and more friendly people who invited him in out of the cold for cookies and conversation.

Olson soon realized that what he was doing could be compared to playing or not playing tape recordings. By refusing to think about the rejections he got, he was preventing a "negative tape" from playing over and over in his mind. By shutting off those negative tapes he was able to hang loose emotionally as he made his sales calls and not get uptight when he got rejected.[1]

Dr. Olson believes that your subconscious mind is a crucial mechanism. If you continue to feed it negative thoughts you get negative results. But, if you feed your subconscious positive thoughts, you get positive results. Your subconscious mind is a powerful tool. You decide how you will use it—against yourself or for your own good.

Negative Tapes Come in All Sizes and Colors

There are all kinds of negative tapes. Dr. Olson mentions the well-known "What if?" tapes, which thrive on fear and worry. People who play "What if?" tapes are very afraid of failure or making mistakes. They say:

"What if they don't come on time?"

"What if I burn the roast?"

"What if it rains?"

Playing "What if?" tapes keeps you nervous, uptight and unsure. When played at their loudest, they can render you practically helpless in a crucial situation. (For example, you think, "What if I mess up this important phone call?" And so you go right ahead and do just that.)

Are you a perfectionist? According to Dr. Olson, perfectionists often play Name Calling tapes which they direct toward themselves, others or the world around them. Name Calling tapes sound like this:

"Now how did you manage that, you *klutz!*"

"We're totally *hopeless*, never get anywhere on time!"

"Yes, 97 is pretty good, but I was a *dummy* to miss those three easy ones!"

Perfectionists chase impossible dreams. Neither they nor those around them can live up to their high standards and strict demands. So, they constantly hear those Name Calling tapes playing in living stereo in each ear. They continually remind themselves that they and the whole cotton pickin' world should be doing better.[2]

There are many other negative tapes we could add to the list. For example:

The "I can't" tape.

The "Why try?" tape.

The "It ain't fair" tape.

And so on, and so on, and so on . . .

How to Erase Your Negative Tapes

We all have our personal set of negative tapes. How then do we break them up? Erase them? Refuse to listen to them?

Dr. Ken Olson believes that anyone who wants to erase his negative tapes must decide that he wants to change and then take personal responsibility for seeing that change does occur. He suggests several good strategies for dealing with negative tapes.

Talk to yourself. As soon as the negative tapes start playing (as soon as you are aware you are thinking those habitual negative thoughts) don't try to ignore them. Instead, challenge them by saying something like: "I'm tired of this garbage." Or, try making fun of your negative thinking: "Yes, what if I blow it? And what if the whole world blows up?"

The idea behind talking to yourself is to make yourself consciously aware of the negative tape you are playing. Then you can see how silly and destructive it is and deal with it. People may give you funny looks if you actually go around muttering things under your breath like "Get outta here!" but it's better than letting those negative tapes play on uninterrupted.

Decide you are in charge. When the negative tapes start to play, ask yourself if you really want to go on feeling miserable and depressed. This technique is especially useful when somebody criticizes you unfairly. Instead of reacting in anger or embarrassment, try seeing the other person as someone with a problem. Just because he has a problem doesn't mean you have to make it yours, too.

Climb out of your rut. Don't continue in your same old patterns. Even if it feels awkward or phony, try behaving differently. For example, if you're shy, try saying hello to at least one new person each day. If you are the kind who comes on too strong, try keeping your mouth shut and letting others have their say. The important thing is to act differently even if you don't feel like it (which you probably won't). The key to getting out of a rut is wanting to, not waiting until you "feel like it." You never will feel like it; you simply have to do it.[3]

All of the above are good ideas, as far as they go. But for the follower of Christ they don't go quite far enough. Does the Christian have any more to go on than techniques for erasing negative thoughts? For example, what can he put in their place?

Use Scripture to Turn On Your Positive Tapes

There is tremendous power in what we believe. As we have seen, if we continue to let nothing but negative messages play over and over in our minds, we will believe them, and the result will be self-doubt, anxiety and low self-esteem. But positive messages—*positive tapes* if you please—do the opposite. When we play positive tapes we are more confident, able to hang loose and our self-esteem rises.

The question, of course, is how do we turn on these positive tapes? Does the Bible give the Christian any clues? Indeed it does. The apostle Paul anticipated Ken Olson's ideas on hanging loose in an uptight world when he wrote to the Philippian Christians and said:

Finally, brethren, whatever is true, whatever is honorable, whatever is right, whatever is pure, whatever is lovely, whatever is of good repute, if there is any excellence and if anything worthy of praise, let your mind dwell on these things (Phil. 4:8).

Right here, in 40 clear words, Paul gives us the recipe for the kind of nutrition we should be feeding our minds every day. Paul knew that the human mind will always dwell on something. We are what we think, and Paul says we should think about:

Things that are true. We don't knowingly put our trust in the false and the phony. We want to count on the things that are reliable and accurate. Unfortunately, many Christians get sucked into believing the lies in various kinds of negative tapes.

Sometimes the messages start in our own heads; sometimes other people lay them on us. But when you make a mistake, don't condemn yourself by saying things like, "You dummy, you always goof" or "You never do things right." Avoid esteem-destroying words like "always" and "never." Instead, say things like: "Well, I tried but I didn't quite make it." Or there's nothing wrong with going to the old cliches like, "Nobody's perfect" (nobody is) and "You can't win 'em all" (you can't). Find the truth about yourself. Don't exaggerate in either direction.

Another idea is to remind yourself of the fantastic truths in the Bible:

"Jesus *does* love me" (warts and all).

"God doesn't expect me to become perfect overnight" (He's very patient).

"The Holy Spirit is at work in me right now" (and He isn't going to go on strike for better conditions).

"I can do anything" (that Christ wants me to).

Things that are honest (or honorable). During the Watergate investigation there was a lot of talk about honor and dishonor. President Richard Nixon and his staff were all charged with destroying America's national honor before the eyes of the world. Even the honor of newly-appointed President Ford was questioned when he pardoned Nixon, while many on Nixon's staff had to stand trial and go to prison.

Many Americans were stunned, baffled and disillu-

87

sioned by Watergate. How could a president and his staff do such a thing? Some people got acute attacks of self-righteousness. They assured themselves that *they* could never act that way.

In her book, *A Gift of Love*, Gail Magruder describes what it was like to see her husband, Jeb, charged and tried for his part in the Watergate crimes. Just before he was to begin serving his prison sentence, the Dick Cavett talk show requested a live television interview with Jeb and his family right in his own home. Gail wanted to refuse, but her husband convinced her to go ahead because the people in the media had a job to do too. Besides, Dick Cavett was considered to be the "gentleman of TV" so all would undoubtedly go well.

With Gail and the Magruder children present, the interview turned out to be what she remembers as "a horrible experience." Instead of using the reams of background material that his studio assistants had gathered on the Magruder family, it seemed to Gail that Dick Cavett made a special point of repeatedly saying that he could never do what Jeb Magruder had done—that he could never "sink that low." Viewers of the show wrote to Gail Magruder later to tell her that Cavett made a fool of himself by "setting himself up as a god."[4]

Gail Magruder's experience during an insensitive TV interview demonstrates that honor is a two-way street. Jeb and Gail Magruder were little more than nominal churchgoers before Watergate, but they made serious commitments to Christ because of their ordeal. During Jeb's time of imprisonment they learned new meanings for the word "honorable."

Just how can a Christian focus in a practical way on doing what is honorable? One approach is to emphasize things that would bring you honor if they were said out loud (or even over television):

"I care about others."

"I go out of my way to help."

"I keep my word."

"I respect the feelings of other people."

What truthful things can you say about yourself that would bring honor? Concentrate on doing those things and making them part of your life.

Things that are right—or just. We all want justice, to be treated fairly. The concept of justice is at the heart of the Golden Rule: "Just as you want men to treat you, treat them in the same way" (Luke 6:31).

When it comes to building healthy self-esteem, be sure you are fair to yourself. Take your fair share of the blame when something goes wrong, but no more than that. To be able to admit you are wrong is a great asset, but don't turn it into a liability by confessing all the world's faults and taking them on yourself.

When Paul wrote to the Philippians, the Greek word he used for "just" was connected to the idea of "doing your duty." You have probably heard a lot about doing your duty to God and others, and so you should. But if you get hung up on playing negative tapes that put yourself down, you really aren't being helpful to anyone. A lot of people go around being unfair to themselves and they call it "humility." To paraphrase the Golden Rule, "Just as you believe others should be treated, be sure to treat yourself the same way" (see Luke 6:31).

Things that are pure and lovely. Paul doesn't mean pure water or pure air, as important as those things are. He means pure morals, pure thoughts. By "lovely" Paul means "that which calls forth love."[5] Hostility, vengeance, bitterness, criticism, jealousy, etc., etc., are not pure and do not call forth love. For the Christian, concentrating on "pure, lovely things" means thinking about your special uniqueness before God. Every Christian is righteous and pure in God's sight because of the tremendous price He paid through Christ's death on the cross. Next time the immoral and the unlovely come your way, just picture Christ standing there with His nail-scarred hands stretching out to you. It could be the best mind cleanser you ever used.

Things that are of good repute, excellent and worthy of praise. Obviously, negative tapes like "What if?", "It ain't fair," and Name Calling don't fit here. The ugly, the false, the questionable tidbit of gossip—none of these build self-esteem; they only tear it down in yourself and others. What Paul is talking about here are things which are "only fit for God to hear."[6] To keep your mind centered on thoughts fit only for God seems like an impossible task, and it is. But the more the Christian can keep his mind on Christ, the closer he will come to this highest of ideals—and to higher self-esteem.

Here is the very bottom line on having a good self-image. You can read books on building sound self-esteem (*The Art of Hanging Loose in an Uptight World* is only one of many good examples).[7] You can try to master their techniques and tips, many of which are excellent. But what the Christian has going for him is something far more powerful and effective. *God, the Holy Spirit, lives in you* (see Rom. 8:9,16; Eph. 3:16)!

So, it doesn't matter if you are just plain ordinary when it comes to looks or ability. It doesn't matter if you lacked status back there in high school—if you never made homecoming queen, cheerleader, nor earned a varsity letter. It doesn't matter if you lack a college degree or a degree from a prestige college. It doesn't matter if your job lacks status or your car lacks power seats and windows. It doesn't even matter if your spouse or your kids or your supervisor are constantly after you about something.

All of that is based on the world's system of values. The world accepts you on its terms and there are always strings (sometimes ropes) attached. The world determines your worth according to your qualities, abilities or performance. It's important to try to succeed in this world, sure, but it shouldn't be what matters most.

What does matter is succeeding at being a person who knows God through Christ. Even if you don't change all that much, even if you never "make it big," you still have God's acceptance and approval. You still have the guarantee and promise:

BECAUSE SOMEBODY LOVES YOU,
YOU ARE INDEED SOMEBODY!

HOW MUCH DO I VALUE MY FAITH?
PART IV

CHAPTER 12

IMPERFECT FEAR CASTS OUT FAITH

In the last several chapters we looked at two very important ideas: how much we value God depends on how close we feel to Christ; how much we value ourselves, depends on how well we understand God's love for us.

So far so good.

Now all we need is the faith to make it work. Funny thing about faith. When we don't need it, we seem to have plenty. But when we run into a problem or a tough situation, our faith often seems to fade faster than a New Year's resolution.

Why is this so? Why can't we just go to our "bank of faith" and withdraw whatever we need for the occasion? If you think about it, the major killer of faith is fear. The Bible tells us "Perfect love casts out fear" (1 John 4:18). Too often we see our imperfect fear casting out the assurance of God's love.

Remember checking off that list of statements in

chapter 4 that best describe you? Most of the people I surveyed on what they wanted most checked "Have a stronger faith in God, Christ." Perhaps you did too.

All Christians "believe," but we wish we could believe more. We are like the father of the boy possessed by a demon. The father told Christ, "If you can do anything, please help us."

"If I can!" replied Jesus. "All things are possible if you only believe."

"I believe," said the father. "Help me in my unbelief." (See Mark 9:14-24.)

Don't you identify with that father? He wanted to believe but he still had doubts. He wanted to trust the Lord completely, but he couldn't quite put it all together. It's the same with us. We say we value God and His Son. We want to believe we can value ourselves because of what God has done for us. We want to feel free of guilt, anxiety and low self-esteem. Christ has told us we can know the truth and the truth can set us free (see John 8:32). But too often we are still hog-tied by fear, shackled by anxiety, handcuffed by worry. Let's face it. We find it easier to doubt than trust, we are more prone to panic than to stand pat with God's promises.

What can we do about this? Where does our faith, or lack of it, fit into our system of values?

Again and again Jesus asked His followers to simply believe. And again and again their fears kept them from doing it. We can learn a lot about what fear does to faith by looking at the well-known report of Peter's walk on the water.

After Jesus finished feeding the 5,000, He sent the disciples on ahead to the other side of the Sea of Galilee while He remained behind to disperse the huge crowd and spend some time alone in prayer.

Later that night the disciples were having a tough

time out on the lake due to high winds and waves. Suddenly they saw Jesus walking toward them on the water! They thought He was a ghost and were almost ready to abandon ship, but Jesus calmed them down by saying:

> *"Take courage, it is I; do not be afraid."* *And Peter answered Him and said, "Lord, if it is You, command me to come to You on the water." And He said, "Come!" And Peter got out of the boat, and walked on the water and came toward Jesus. But seeing the wind, he became afraid, and beginning to sink, he cried out, saying, "Lord, save me!" And immediately Jesus stretched out His hand and took hold of him, and said to him, "O you of little faith, why did you doubt?" And when they got into the boat, the wind stopped. And those who were in the boat worshiped Him, saying, "You are certainly God's Son!"* (Matt. 14:27-33).

This story is a perfect example of the kind of fellow Peter was—impulsive, always ready to act first and think afterwards. He just stepped out of the boat and started walking toward his Lord.

But then he started looking around at the wind and waves. The thought struck him: "*What* am I doing out here? I must be crazy!" And as fear gripped him, Peter started to sink.

What happened next shows us something else about Peter. He could get into trouble by acting on impulse, but he also knew where to go when things got tough. "Lord, save me!" is often the best prayer we can utter at certain moments, and that's exactly what Peter shouted. Jesus responded by reaching down and giving Peter a hand and a mild rebuke. "Why, Peter, did you have such little faith? Why did you doubt?"

The obvious answer is that Peter became afraid. Never did anyone start out with more faith. Never did anyone start to sink faster because of fear. A standard explanation of this story is that as long as Peter had his eyes on the Lord, he was in good shape. The minute he took his eyes off Jesus, however, and started noticing how high the waves were and how hard the wind was blowing, he was in big trouble. The same thing, goes the explanation, can happen to us today. If we take our eyes off Christ and start thinking about the situation, the pressure, the problems, we go down to defeat.

The analogy is helpful, but it doesn't completely solve our problem. For one thing, as miraculous and spectacular as Peter's walk on the water was, he was looking right at Christ and he had heard Jesus say that he could come to Him on the water. And, when Peter started to sink, he could cry out to Christ Himself, reach for Christ's hand and be lifted up. In other words, Peter could exercise faith in what he could see and touch. Today, Christians must exercise faith in what they cannot see or touch. "Faith," says the writer to the Hebrews, "is the assurance of things hoped for, the conviction of things not seen" (Heb. 11:1).

So, in a way, even out there in the middle of the Sea of Galilee, without water skis, surfboard or life jacket, Peter had it easier than we do today. We hope for things but we don't always seem to have quite enough "blessed assurance." We have our convictions but we wish we could walk by sight at least part of the way in the tough situations. Fortunately, Jesus is as patient with us as He was with Peter—possibly more so. He reaches down, lifts us up and says:

WHY DO YOU DOUBT?
IT IS I . . . BE NOT AFRAID.

GOT ALL THE FAITH YOU NEED, DEAR?

If you could manufacture faith and sell it, you would soon have a multimillion dollar business going. Think of the possibilities. Faith in liquid form for those who needed a small glass every four hours. Faith in tiny time capsules that lasted up to 12 hours. Faith in giant megatablets for the really big problem or crisis.

But faith doesn't work that way. Faith isn't something we buy. It's a gift we receive and it's also something we do. Faith is *what* we believe—the truths of Scripture. Faith is *how* we believe—the degree of our ability to rest in the Lord, trust Him, hope in Him and cleave (hang on) to Him.

Take a Look at "What" You Believe

We don't have a lot of trouble with the "what" kind of faith. Or do we? Take the following quiz to get a better picture of how your faith might stand up to typical pressures today. Check the answer that comes closest to how you would respond to each situation. Don't take a lot of time to decide which answer is the "most spiritual." Simply give your first response as honestly as you can.

Somebody comes up and asks you, "Why believe in God? What are you getting out of it?" You think:

a.____Where would I be without Him? I get everything out of it!

b.____Wonder why she's asking that? My religion is my business.

c.____I'm not sure. Wish I *knew* what I was getting out of it.

You and a friend are talking. She remarks: "I don't see how you can go to that church. I know for a fact that a lot of the teenagers there are hypocrites—they run with the wildest bunch in town." Your first thought is:

a.____There are some wild kids in our church group, but God can change them.

b.____Where does she come off talking about my church? Every church has hypocrites!

c.____I guess she's right. I wish those kids didn't come to our church. They're giving us a bad image!

An acquaintance comments: "I can't buy this 'Christ died for our sins' bit. It's too easy to just believe and be saved. You have to earn what you get in this world." Your response is to:

a.____Explain that Christ had to die for our sins because we cannot match God's standards ourselves. No one can earn his salvation, but Christians serve Christ out of love and gratitude.

b.____Tell this person he ought to try reading the Bible; then get out of there, fast.

99

c.____Change the subject, explaining that everyone has a right to his own beliefs.

Your pastor preaches an inspiring sermon on the value of Bible reading and study. Your response is to:
a.____Renew your determination to spend more time in Scripture.
b.____Be a little irked with your pastor for preaching the same old stuff when there are so many important issues to discuss.
c.____Yawn.

A Christian you have known for a long time surprises you by expressing doubts about the effectiveness of prayer. "Lately I pray but God just doesn't answer," Harry says. "Does it really do any good? God knows what's going to happen anyway." You think:
a.____We don't pray primarily to get answers. We pray to talk to God and share our lives with Him.
b.____What's the matter with Harry? He must be losing his faith.
c.____Now that I think of it, I have a lot of unanswered prayers. I wonder—

There are no right or wrong answers to a quiz like this. It simply describes various responses to various situations or questions. Obviously, however, the *a* answers sound more confident, more full of faith. If you honestly checked the *a* answer at least four times, your faith is in fairly good shape as far as the "what" is concerned. You have a nondefensive yet confident approach to following Christ and you have a good grasp on basic beliefs about Jesus, salvation, sin, the Bible and prayer. You may not be totally fearless, but you are trusting God to guide you.

If you checked quite a few of the *b* responses (or at least leaned that way), better stop to think. You may be a prime candidate for becoming a defensive Christian who is willing to give assent to doctrines but doesn't know how to cope with opposition and doubting. Fear can make us critical or defensive.

If you came up with several checks that were closer to the *c* category, you may have a serious problem with the amount of knowledge you have of Christianity or your understanding of the gospel. Many Christians aren't sure what they believe. Their response to pressure is fear, or sometimes apathy.

What About "How" You Believe?

What we believe is only part of our faith picture. *How* we believe—our actions and responses—is equally important. Try this next quiz to see where you stand on the "how" of faith.

You agree the Bible is the Christian's only real primary source of information and as a regular practice you:

a.____Seldom read it.

b.____Try to read all the newest commentaries and other Christian books to see what the outstanding authors are saying.

c.____Try to read the Bible at least several times a week.

You agree that Christ is the only answer to the world's problems and you:

a.____Seldom share your faith because you don't want to offend anyone.

b.____Try to witness to several people each day because you know you should.

c.____Try to share your faith in every way you can because you want to.

101

You agree that prayer is important, if not vital, to Christian living. During the week you make several important decisions, have two major disagreements with your spouse, and have to bawl out the kids several times. As you look back on the week, what part did prayer play in what you said or did?

a.____Come to think of it, I only prayed when I got in a real spot.

b.____I tried to pray, but usually acted on my own and hoped it would work out.

c.____I usually remembered to pray, not only for guidance but to offer praise and thanksgiving.

You agree Christians should be kind and loving. Your response to others is usually based on:

a.____How they treat me.

b.____How things work out.

c.____How I can best help them.

You hear that one of your best friends said something derogatory behind your back. You decide you will:

a.____Scratch him (or her) off your list.

b.____Act as if nothing happened, but keep close tabs on this friend in the future, to see if it happens again.

c.____Confront your friend, even if it's difficult, and set things straight.

Like the first quiz, this one is set up to give you an idea of how you might respond to certain situations or problems. In this case, however, the c responses are the ones that would show the most faith. If you can unhesitatingly say that your first reaction was to check four or five of the c answers, you are on the right track concerning the "how" end of faith. Your actions are more likely to back up what you say you believe.

If you find yourself with quite a few of the *b* responses you could be sliding into that twilight zone where your faith is something you say you believe, but seldom something you do with enthusiasm. If you serve Christ at all, it's more out of fear and guilt than love and obedience.

If several *a* responses popped up in your answers, you definitely have a problem with putting together Christian practice and principle. Go back and re-examine what you believe. Faith has to start with *what* we believe, but if the *what* doesn't affect how we live, it is little more than mental gymnastics. On the other hand, too much *how* and not enough *what* can lead to faith that is empty or even foolish. (For example, you can try driving down a residential street at 75 m.p.h. and have "faith" nothing will happen, but the police won't be too happy.)

If our faith is to conquer our fears, we need balance between what we believe and how we live out those beliefs.

No, faith doesn't come in bottles or capsules. Faith isn't something you can take; faith is something you use and, like a muscle, the more you use faith the stronger it becomes.

Nor is faith free-floating and ethereal. Faith must have an object and that object is Jesus Christ. Faith grows stronger as you live, move and act—as you trust Christ with the good and bad of each day.

TO HAVE ALL THE FAITH YOU NEED
KNOW CHRIST AS BEST YOU CAN.

CHAPTER 14

YOU PACK YOUR OWN CHUTE!

As the last two chapters told us, faith is one of the Christian's most treasured values. And like many treasures, your faith is in need of constant maintenance and repair. In a way, it is always "under construction."

A simple, but not simplistic, approach to building your faith is a plan developed in the book *Recycled for Living*, by Earl G. Lee, pastor of the First Nazarene Church, Pasadena, California. Pastor Lee got his idea from Psalm 37:1-7 (note that the key words appear in caps):

FRET NOT yourself because of evildoers,
Be not envious toward wrongdoers.
For they will wither quickly like the grass,
And fade like the green herb.
TRUST in the Lord, and do good;
Dwell in the land and cultivate faithfulness.

DELIGHT yourself in the Lord;
And He will give you the desires of your heart.
 COMMIT your way to the Lord,
Trust also in Him, and He will do it.
And He will bring forth your righteousness as
the light,
And your judgment as the noonday.
 REST in the Lord and wait patiently for
Him;
Fret not yourself because of him who prospers
in his way,
Because of the man who carries out wicked
schemes.

As the first two words of Psalm 37:1 put it: *fret not.* Stop fussing and worrying so much. Pastor Lee compares worrying to gunning your engine while parked in neutral. You make a lot of noise and smoke but don't go anywhere. He believes that legitimate concern is something entirely different from worry. When you are rightfully concerned about something, you do something about it. You put your car in gear, so to speak, and get rolling.[1]

If you are a chronic worrier, there is no instant cure. It isn't as simple as saying, "Worry is a sin, so I guess I better stop that." People who are eaten up by worry would stop if they could, but they're trapped. Some of them have made such a habit of worry that they actually enjoy it in a way. At least, they prefer to worry. Others are so full of fears and anxieties they can't do anything but worry. Some of us are like Charlie Brown who told Lucy, "I worry about my worrying so much . . . that my anxieties have anxieties."[2]

If you want to use Pastor Lee's cycle of faith approach, your first step is to stop *fretting*. To stop *fretting* you have to make a conscious decision not to let things

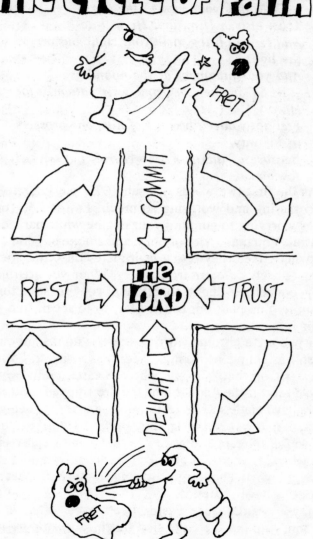

get to you. You can do that by *committing* yourself to Christ. Yes, you have heard that one before, but Pastor Lee has a new twist. As a missionary in India, he learned the Marathi language. In Marathi, a free translation of "Commit your way to the Lord" would be "Turn what you are and what you have over to God—palms down!" In other words, don't knowingly bring along any hidden hang-ups or agendas. Whatever the problem, you don't just say, "Here, Lord, take it." Instead, you say, "Here, Lord, I let it go!" There is a *big* difference.[3]

Trust is the next step. Someone once asked Pastor Lee: "I've committed everything, including myself, to the Lord. Now what do I do?"

He replied, "There is only one thing to do, lean hard! . . . You don't just lean; you lean on Someone well able to carry your weight."[4]

That "Someone well able to carry" our weight is God, but we seem to be able to trust other things with our weight more easily than we do the Lord. We use chairs, bridges, walkways, escalators and elevators with nary a qualm. But when it comes to trusting God with a problem, it seems harder.

One helpful idea came from Diane, a member of a group I talked with while researching this book. She pointed out: "Sometimes we try trusting too much at one time. For example, a little girl would probably be afraid to jump out of a 10-foot tree into her daddy's arms. But she might be willing to try jumping off a one-foot rock and let her daddy catch her. So often we hear we should trust God with everything, and I agree we should. But our faith isn't always that strong. Some of us might do better to take some smaller steps of faith and then work up to 'everything.' "

Following trust comes *delight*. The psalmist tells us to delight ourselves in the Lord and He will give us what we want (see Ps. 37:4). Sounds too good to be true, and a little questionable, too. We may have heard from our pastor or other spiritual advisors that getting what you want (the desires of your heart) isn't always so good. We may want the wrong things or perhaps we require too much of a good thing. So, why does the psalmist give us this promise?

For one thing, if you have sincerely committed yourself to God and are trusting Him, there will be an automatic check on what you desire. As Saint Augustine put it so well: "Love God, and do as you please."

But what if things are going sour? Is the promise in Psalm 37:4 any good then? Of course. What the psalmist is saying is that we should praise God in *all* things. If we are praising God sincerely, we will find that what we have is good enough because God is with us. Praise brings joy and satisfaction, even when things aren't going all that well.

Finally, according to the cycle of faith, we are to *rest* in Christ. Does that sound like being ready for retirement or beyond? Not necessarily. We all need to rest now and then. Pastor Lee likes to use the word "cycle" when referring to living by faith because he believes that "life actually seems to move in cycles. It seems that we no sooner handle one problem or one situation than another one arises."[5] We are tempted to fret and fume. We can decide to commit, then trust and finally delight —praise God for working in us. After all that, we have earned a little rest.

Granted, the times for rest may be brief or seemingly nonexistent. Just as an experienced runner or backpacker learns to pace himself physically, we have to learn to pace ourselves spiritually. Next time things get hectic, try praying this paraphrase of Psalm 23:1:

Lord, you are my Pacesetter; I shall not rush.

We All Pack Our Own Chutes

Pastor Lee's cycle of faith sounds good. It makes sense and it all can work, but it is not a magic formula. He cautions that at any time fretting can pull you out of the cycle. Fortunately, God is gracious. Getting pulled out of the cycle doesn't disqualify you from getting back in. You simply commit yourself again, and keep trusting, delighting and resting. It's strictly up to you as to how long you stay in the cycle of faith and how long you let fretting keep you out of it.

Building our faith and tearing down our fears depends on using the freedom of will God has given to each of us. We choose freely how we will act or think. Nobody chooses for us.

Eden Ryle, vivacious and dynamic teacher of motivational skills and techniques, emphasizes this freedom to choose in her classes and lectures. She believes we create a lot of our own unrealistic fears, such as being afraid we will be rejected. For example, she knew many salesmen who would decide not to make that call on an important client because "It just isn't the right time of day," or "He's too busy, better try tomorrow."

While searching for just the right example to explain her theories, Eden happened to attend an air show. For the first time in her life, she saw a "live" parachute jump and a sky diver floated to a perfect landing right in front of her. She talked to the parachutist and asked him if he were ever afraid. He replied that he had nothing to fear. "After all," he said, "I pack my own chute."

The "pack my own chute" phrase stuck in Eden's mind and she decided to investigate further. She discovered that sky divers do pack their own chutes, carefully folding them in just the right way so they will not snarl or jam when they pull the rip cord. She quickly saw a comparison between packing your own parachute and how we all move through life. All of us "pack our own chutes" as we choose how we will think or act.

Although the idea of jumping out of an airplane terrified her, Eden decided she would take instruction and make a jump, just to prove that our fears do not have to paralyze us. She took several hours of instruction at a jump school and her fears multiplied. The plan called for jumping into the Pacific Ocean. Landing on water was supposed to be safer than landing on the ground, but would the chute come down on top of her? Would she get entangled and drown? Would sharks attack? Would she be able to pull the rip cord at the right moment? Would the pick-up boat be able to find her? (She couldn't swim and a life jacket was ruled out as impractical while she was wearing the parachute.)

Finally the big day came. The weather was perfect so there was no turning back. The plane reached altitude and Eden climbed out on the wing strut as the wind whipped into her face from the spinning prop only a few feet away. She pushed off into space and her chute opened. Her splashdown was perfect. The chute did not cover her, the sharks did not come and the boat was right there to pick her up. She conquered her fears and was able to function, even though she was terrified throughout the entire experience.[6]

You Function in Spite of Fears

Eden Ryle saw her first parachute jump as a symbol of the fears that haunt everyone in one way or another. We are all afraid of something and our fears can become overwhelming if we don't cope with them. For example, we fear competition because we fear failing or being defeated. We fear being told no and we fear being made to feel inadequate. We fear criticism and we fear the unknown (like parachute jumps). All of these fears are unrealistic, but they can still be very real to the person who has them.

The key to faith is to function even though you are afraid; and depend on God for the outcome. Being able to function depends on your attitude and outlook. Every day is like a jump from a plane. We jump (some of us roll or stagger) out of bed in the morning and by night-fall we land on our feet—or somewhere else. It all depends on how we have mentally packed our own chutes.

A Christian packs his own chute by allowing Christ to control his feelings and behavior. Instead of going into a fret tailspin we can stop and take stock. We can choose to continue fretting, or we can commit ourselves to Christ and trust Him, just as a parachutist commits himself to his chute and trusts it to bring him to safety.

Challenges, problems and fear are part of life. But if there weren't something to be afraid of or concerned about, there would be no need for faith. So, stop fretting. Commit yourself to Christ. Trust Him and praise Him (fears and all). It's your choice:

FRET IT OR FAITH IT,
YOU PACK YOUR OWN CHUTE.

PART V

CHAPTER 15

LOVE, HONOR AND BE SURE TO STAY

As we hear continually about friends and acquaintances who are divorced—or getting divorced—[1] the questions continue to haunt us:

Why doesn't marriage work better?

What does it take to keep a marriage together?

What does it take to put a little zap into a marriage?

Answers to these questions and dozens more on the mystery of marriage can be found in bookstores across the land. Just a sampling of book titles devoted to making marriage work include:

How to Be the Wife of a Happy Husband

Total Woman

Total Man

What Wives Wish Their Husbands Knew About Women

What Every Woman Should Know About a Man

Forever My Love

Communication: Key to Your Marriage

How to Be Happy, Though Married
The Act of Marriage
Do Yourself a Favor: Love Your Wife
Thoroughly Married
Discovering the Intimate Marriage

What is significant, if not startling, about the above list is that every book is written by a Christian author, primarily to help Christians make marriage work. If marriage is an "institution ordained by God," why are an alarming number of Christian marriages in trouble or at least dull and unhappy?

To keep a marriage alive and well do you prize and cherish your partner? Do you prize and cherish marriage itself? Or is it quite a bit of both?

What Did Jesus Say About Marriage?

Jesus didn't give any lengthy discourses on marriage counseling, but what He did say got right to the heart of what marriage is and why it should be a lasting proposition:

> *And some Pharisees came to Him, testing Him, and saying, "Is it lawful for a man to divorce his wife for any cause at all?"*
>
> *And He answered and said, "Have you not read, that He who created them from the beginning made them male and female, and said, 'For this cause a man shall leave his father and mother, and shall cleave to his wife; and the two shall become one flesh'? Consequently they are no more two, but one flesh. What therefore God has joined together, let no man separate."*
>
> *They said to Him, "Why then did Moses command to give her a certificate and divorce her?"*

> *He said to them, "Because of your hardness of heart, Moses permitted you to divorce your wives; but from the beginning it has not been this way. And I say to you, whoever divorces his wife, except for immorality, and marries another commits adultery"* (Matt. 19:3-9).

Matthew reports that the Pharisees came to Jesus to "test" Him (v. 3). Again and again they asked Jesus questions designed to trap Him. This was no exception. What they wanted to know was a major topic of debate in Israel in those days: "Is it lawful for a man to divorce his wife for any cause at all?"

At that time the rabbis were divided into two schools of thought concerning divorce. One school, led by the famous rabbi named Shammai, said the only legitimate reason for divorce was adultery. The other school, led by an equally famous rabbi named Hillel, said that just about anything was sufficient cause for divorce—even burning breakfast or getting a few too many wrinkles.

The followers of Shammai and Hillel argued constantly over the interpretation of Deuteronomy 24:1:

> *When a man hath taken a wife, and married her, and it come to pass that she find no favor in his eyes, because he hath found some uncleanness in her: then let him write her a bill of divorcement, and give it in her hand, and send her out of his house (KJV).*

The main argument centered around the words, "some uncleanness." The conservatives (followers of Shammai) said "some uncleanness" referred only to an act of sexual unfaithfulness—adultery. The liberals (followers of Hillel) argued that "some uncleanness" could mean just about any fault a husband might find in his wife. One rabbi even taught that if a wife "found no favor in her husband's eyes," it meant he could divorce

116

her because he had met another woman who was prettier.[2]

Obviously, the freewheeling ideas of Hillel were more popular than the rigid opinions of Shammai—at least among Jewish *men*. In Israel at that time women were treated as little more than slaves. In the eyes of Jewish law, a woman was a thing, the possession of her father or her husband, with few legal rights. If a man wanted to write his wife a bill of divorcement there was little she could do about it. By facing Jesus with this question of divorce the Pharisees were putting Him in a delicate spot. No matter how He answered, some people would disagree with Him. And if He did not go along with the liberal ideas taught by Hillel He would be bucking popular opinion.

As we saw in the chapter on decision making, Jesus could care less about popular opinion. He cared only about the truth of God's Word. That is why He went right back to the first mention of marriage in Scripture. God, said Jesus, created male and female (see Gen. 1:27). A man shall leave his parents and cleave to his wife. The two of them shall become as one and what God has joined no man should separate (see Gen. 2:24).

The Pharisees were hung up on the laws and legalities of who could get divorced for what reason. Jesus was interested in establishing the principle of marriage—two joined as one, allowing nothing to come between.

The Pharisees thought they had Jesus in a corner. After all, Moses, the great lawgiver of God, said in Deuteronomy 24:1 that divorce was allowed. Was Jesus trying to say He knew more than Moses?

The answer to that, said Jesus, is that Moses didn't command divorce; he permitted it as a means of helping the Israelites of his day straighten out the terrible mess they had made out of marriage. Things were so bad that

117

men were divorcing their wives for no reason at all. By installing the "bill of divorcement" Moses actually gave women a form of protection because the husband was required to state before two witnesses the reason he was divorcing her. Without a bill of divorcement a woman was wide open to charges of adultery, which could lead to being stoned to death. Instead of making it easy to get a divorce, Moses' bill of divorcement law actually made it more difficult. It guided the Israelite people back toward the original ideal of a lasting marriage with man and woman as one flesh, unseparated by anyone or anything.[3]

But by Jesus' time many of the Pharisees had managed to corrupt God's Word with their own interpretations, additions and deletions. They claimed that the law of Moses *commanded* a man to divorce his wife under "certain conditions." Siding with the liberal teachings of Hillel, they had decided that the idea of "some uncleanness" from Deuteronomy 24:1 could be just about anything the husband wanted it to be. So, the problem Moses tried to solve had come full circle. Once again, women were being treated badly at the whim of their husbands.

As usual, Jesus set the Pharisees straight on just what the Scriptures really say. Marriage, said Jesus, is something that should last for life and the only reason for dissolving it is unfaithfulness on the part of one or both partners. The one who commits adultery breaks the bond of one flesh, and divorce is permissible but not absolutely demanded. It is the choice of the party who has been betrayed.

God's Ideal: Two Stay One

In His teaching on marriage and divorce Jesus gave tremendously high ideals at which to aim. To our permissive, do-your-own-thing society His teachings may sound like unrealistic legalism. But Jesus isn't laying down laws, He is laying down a principle that is based on the first recorded marriage in history. The union of Adam and Eve was a symbol—better yet, a model—by which all marriages were to be measured. God made Eve for Adam and brought her to him:

> *"This is it!" Adam exclaimed. "She is part of my own bone and flesh! Her name is 'woman' because she was taken out of man." This explains why a man leaves his father and mother and is joined to his wife in such a way that the two become one person* (Gen. 2:23,24, TLB).

The concept of "one person" is where every marriage should start and never end. To divide "one person" is to create two partial people. Divorce happens. Jesus was not ignoring that, but what He was saying is that divorce always leaves scars and brokenness. Divorce may happen because human beings are fallible sinners, but God's ideal is lasting marriage.

To go back to the questions asked earlier, with Jesus it wasn't a case of choosing to prize and cherish your partner or choosing to prize and cherish marriage. The Christian is to prize and cherish *both*.

FOR LIFE IN YOUR MARRIAGE
MARRY FOR LIFE

CHAPTER 16

ARE YOU OLD ENOUGH TO BE MARRIED?

When it comes to marriage, there is a basic question to ask yourself, whether you're engaged, a newlywed, or quite a few years down the marriage road:

Am I old enough to be married? Not old enough in years, but old enough in mental, emotional and spiritual ways. In other words, am I mature in my marriage relationship? Immaturity (childishness) probably plagues all marriages to some degree. One definition of many marriages might be two immature people trying to "grow up" together. And it *is* hard to grow up. Childish habits, traits and personality quirks hang on in many of us and surface in our adult years in strange and unique ways.

Take a Look at Your Maturity Level

How mature/childish are you? Following are 10 questions to test your maturity—or the lack of it. The questions are designed to give you absolute freedom. You may cheat all you want to and you may be as honest as you like. No one will ever be the wiser except, perhaps, your spouse. In fact it might be a helpful experiment to take the test for each other as well as for yourselves and then compare answers.

- I want my own way

1	2	3	4	5	6	7	8	9	10
always									never

The childish person wants his own way, right now and the word "compromise" is not in his vocabulary. There is perhaps no relationship that demands the ability to compromise as much as marriage does. Surely it demands that each partner give in to the other in various situations. The opposite of compromise is ultimatum. "If you don't want to do it my way, I'll—(sulk, withhold sex, go home to mother, get a divorce, etc.)." To word the question another way, "Do I try to please myself, my spouse or both of us?"

- I am cruel to my spouse

1	2	3	4	5	6	7	8	9	10
always									never

Cruelty can be physical or mental. Children are often cruel to one another as they tease, hit or call each other names. The same things go on in marriage, usually in more sophisticated form. There is always the possibility of the battered wife (and in some marriages the battered husband), but in a lot of homes, particularly Christian ones, striking each other is considered too crude. Instead, the partners resort to cutting remarks, put-downs, nagging, silence, etc. Other nonviolent ways to be cruel include neglecting your spouse for a hobby, an activity, or longer hours on the job. Cruelty comes in many forms and packages. To word the question another way, "When and how do I withhold kindness, gentleness and concern from my spouse?"

• I engage in self-pity

1	2	3	4	5	6	7	8	9	10
always									never

Children are always feeling sorry for themselves. Their playmates are unfair. Mommy is mean. Daddy is too strict. Teachers are cranky. Adults are more subtle, but still filled with the same basic problems of sulking, martyrdom, melancholy, etc. In a marriage that is being corroded by self-pity you will hear remarks like:

"You don't love me."

"If you cared about me you'd never say that."

"Why do I always have to clean up the mess? Am I the maid?"

"Doesn't anybody care that I work all day and would like a little peace?"

To word the question another way, "How much sympathy do I spend on myself in comparison to my spouse and other family members?"

• I seek revenge

1	2	3	4	5	6	7	8	9	10
always									never

Children get revenge on each other by lashing out physically or verbally. They also get revenge on adults by refusing to eat, sulking, pouting and doing poorly in school. In teenage years they may run away, take drugs or engage in promiscuous sex.

We have also discovered that at a later time in life husbands and wives can continue these childish patterns. The deep freeze (in bed and out), the silent treatment, refusing to get something fixed and noncooperation in any shape and form are just a few vengeance-taking techniques applied maliciously in some marriages. To word the question differently, "When I'm unhappy with my spouse do I 'get back' at him or her in subtle or not so subtle ways?"

122

- I admit faults and mistakes

1	2	3	4	5	6	7	8	9	10
never									always

Children seldom are eager to confess mistakes or wrong-doing because they fear punishment. They often resort to lies, half-truths and other forms of misrepresentation to "get out of it." In many marriages the pattern continues. Husbands and wives are often prone to cover their faults, to be unwilling to admit their mistakes. We prefer to play psychological games like, "You got me into this!" and "Now see what you made me do!"[1] One way to gauge yourself on this question is to think about how often you find yourself saying, "I was wrong," "I goofed," or "I'm sorry."

- I am hostile and quarrelsome

1	2	3	4	5	6	7	8	9	10
always									never

Children bicker and quarrel as a matter of course. Adults, theoretically, do not. Yet, many marriages are continual battle zones or, at best, scenes of tense, temporary truce before the next skirmish breaks out. If husband and wife have both failed to outgrow the childish habit of quarreling, the predictable result is chaos in their home. When one mate is mature enough to avoid quarreling, the other may take it as a sign of weakness and try bullying, picking fights, goading, etc. Another way to look at this question is to ask yourself: "How often do I find myself 'sticking up for my rights,' especially at home?"

- I am responsible

1	2	3	4	5	6	7	8	9	10
never									always

Responsibility is a trait parents try to teach their children with varying amounts of frustration and success. Teaching Johnny to hang up his clothes or Jenny to do her homework before watching television takes patience and perseverance. If Johnny doesn't learn to pick up his clothes as a child, his wife will probably have to do it after he is married. If Jenny fails to see the need to do homework before watching television, she will probably fail to do housework, errands, or other chores before watching the soap opera when she is married. How responsible are you? Another way to ask the question is: "Do I put the routine chores, errands, duties of life ahead of my convenience or pleasure?"

- I am fair

1	2	3	4	5	6	7	8	9	10
never									always

We like to think we are "always fair" but we see fairness through our own eyes, not the eyes of others. Children are typically fair to themselves first and then to others, if it's convenient or doesn't cost anything. In marriage it is difficult to be fair in many situations because of the great emotional investment by both husband and wife. We want to be fair to our mates, but our own interests and needs often creep in.

For example, at day's end the husband comes home weary from fighting with bosses and freeways and he would like to relax before dinner. But the wife has had a hard day too with the kids, a cranky neighbor and an uncooperative oven. Each has a very good idea how the other can be "fair" or "unfair."

Another way to ask this question is, "Am I fair only when the emotional price is low or can I be fair when my own needs, goals and plans are at stake?"

- My feelings control me

1	2	3	4	5	6	7	8	9	10
always									never

A key trait in most children is to do what they feel like doing rather than acting out of obedience or commitment to principles and standards. One of the deadly enemies of marriage today is the prevailing philosophy of "do your own thing" and "if it feels good, do it." Husbands and wives who operate with either of these slogans as a guide are headed for trouble or already have plenty of it.

The well-known stereotype of the husband who spends too much time "doing his own thing" at work or while out with the boys is legendary. And, especially in recent years, the woman's movement has encouraged some wives to abandon the kitchen and laundry room to go do their "own thing" while their husbands and children make do with TV dinners and dirty sox.

Another way to phrase the question is, "What really runs my life? My emotions or my commitment to biblical principles and my mate?"

- I care about my spouse

1	2	3	4	5	6	7	8	9	10
never									always

Children tend to be self-centered, caring only or mostly for themselves. Hopefully, as they grow up they gain the ability to care about others. A lot of adults, however, marry without the conviction or commitment to care for their mates. Instead, they want to be cared for, and the fight is on:

"Well, if you had any consideration—"

"It seems to me that I deserve a little more—"

"All I'm asking is—"

"I always want *my* way? What about *you*?"

A different way to think of this question is, "In my marriage am I self-centered or mate-centered?"

Scoring code—In general, the higher you score on each question the more mature a marriage partner you should be. There is no "passing grade" for this kind of quiz. It is only an informal tool to help you think about how you are relating to your mate in some very important areas. If you think your score may be too high, ask your spouse to grade you on each question. It will be a great way to test your maturity!

Marriage Is Much More than Fun and Games

One of the acid tests of anyone's maturity level is how he or she handles frustration and disappointment. We expect so much from life (and especially marriage) but we usually get something quite different.

Rubin Carson, author of the best-selling paperback, *The National Love, Sex and Marriage Test*, observes that the typical American brings dozens of expectations into marriage and when those expectations are "brutally dashed on the shores of reality," the marriage often starts to crumble.[2] According to Carson, some of those expectations are:

That a good marriage is as perfect and romantic as the courtship was;

That a good marriage relationship never has any hassles or arguments;

That in a good marriage sex will always be available and totally satisfying;

That the ability to communicate magically starts the moment you get married. ("If you love me, I shouldn't have to tell you.");

That emotional security is an automatic benefit for both marriage partners.[3]

Author Carson takes 170 pages, including the opinions of nationally known marriage and family specialists and the scores of thousands who took the national love, sex and marriage test, to show that between marriage expectations and marriage realities there is a great gulf fixed. To bridge that gulf, more couples must march to the altar knowing that at best they face equal amounts of challenge and difficulty along with all of the advertised joy and bliss. Marriage has a lot more to offer than fun and games. It presents the opportunity to grow out of the self-centeredness of childhood to become functioning adults who know what it means to give, to suffer, to work together to build a relationship that glorifies God. Paul was speaking primarily of the church, but his words fit the Christian marriage perfectly: "Speaking the truth in love, we are to grow up in all aspects into Him, who is the head, even Christ" (Eph. 4:15).

NO MATTER HOW OLD YOU ARE
MARRIAGE IS FOR ADULTS ONLY.

CHAPTER 17

If you read only the marriage books suggested in the opening of chapter 15, you could find dozens—if not hundreds—of ideas to put into action in your marriage. Most of these ideas can be traced back to basic principles for building good relationships. Three of those basic principles are: *caring, communicating, being constructive.*

What Does It Mean to "Care"?

Dr. Dwight Small, author, lecturer and counselor in the field of marriage, believes that describing a couple's successful togetherness as "love" is being too unspecific. But describing a marriage relationship as "caring" is to give some tangible and useful meaning to the general idea of love.

To care is to put the abstract word, love, into action. One way to say it would be: "Caring puts a handle on love."[1] Romance and sexual attraction are obviously a part of falling in love and getting married, but *caring* is what will make the marriage go—and last.

Following are some questions to help you see how big a part caring plays in your marriage.

Do I care enough to want the best for my mate? The secular world's value system often says, "Go ahead, use the other person to get what you want." A caring Christian loves the person, not things. Marriage offers the ultimate opportunity to love the person, not things.

To apply these ideas to your own marriage ask yourself: "Do I value my mate for what I can get or what I can give?"

When I look at my mate do I see a person or a performer (is my love for my mate conditioned by what he or she *does* or by who he or she *is?*)

Am I interested in controlling my mate or in liberating him or her? (What have I done lately to free my mate to take a job, to have time away from the children, to engage in a favorite hobby, to grow and become the person God intends him or her to be?)

Beware, though, because caring can be difficult. Sometimes (often?) when we try to care for someone it either backfires or we don't get much of a response back. It's easy to care for others when they respond in turn. We say we believe the Golden Rule—doing unto others as we would have them do unto us. Actually, life teaches us to do unto others and then wait for them to pay us back!

If you're committed to caring, Christ will be your model. He came not to be cared for, but to care (see Matt. 20:28). He came not to be served but to be a servant (see Luke 22:26).

Do I care enough to cooperate? That is, am I willing to give in and put my spouse's interests ahead of my own? This doesn't mean being a doormat, but it does call

129

for empathy—putting yourself in your mate's shoes, trying to see how he or she feels. Opportunities to do this are innumerable:

When planning an outing, vacation, etc., give your spouse equal time in suggesting what to do and where to go (especially if you are the well-organized, strongly-opinionated type).

If you know cracking your knuckles (or some other weird little habit you have) drives your mate nuts, don't do it.

Be on time—for appointments, social functions, whatever. Stealing time from others (particularly your mate) by being fashionably or unfashionably late is a sure sign you are more interested in yourself than you are in him or her.

What Is Communication?

In a film that was popular several years ago, the plot revolved around a strong-willed character named Luke who wound up on a prison work farm. He was told the rules and warned about what would happen if he tried to escape. But repeatedly he rebelled and attempted to get away.

In one memorable scene Luke breaks the rules again and the guards lay him low. As he lies in the dirt, dazed from the beating, the prison warden walks up and utters a line that has been more memorable than the film: "What we have here is a failure to communicate!"

The warden believed that the best way to communicate with rebellious prisoners was to beat them into submission. This is one way to "communicate." Marriages, however, do not thrive on this approach.

Communication is not the domination or intimidation of one party by the other. Real communication occurs when two parties equally respect and care for each other. They share information in such a way that they both understand what the other is saying. Talking, listening and understanding are all involved in real communication.[2]

Here are some tips to prevent "failure to communicate."

Open the lines. Make it as easy as you possibly can for others to communicate with you. Contrary to popular opinion, communication doesn't start with being willing to send messages; it starts with being willing to *receive* them. How easy is it to communicate with you?

Am I touchy, irritable, easily hurt? If so, my mate will shy away from being honest with me. In fact, he or she may shy away, period.

Am I willing to admit I was wrong, that I made a mistake? Some of the hardest words for any of us to say are: "I was wrong, I'm sorry."

Do I use silence as a weapon or perhaps as a place to hide? Communication grinds to a halt in a hurry when one party clams up.

Listen up, which is probably the toughest part of communicating. We all love to send messages, but we aren't so fond of listening to messages sent to us. How do you rate as a listener?

Do I look right at my mate when he or she is talking to try to detect feelings as well as hear words?

Do I often find myself thinking of what I'm going to say next rather than concentrating on what is being said to me? (This is particularly easy to do if you are disagreeing or arguing.)

Do I listen objectively or do I tend to read into things that are said to me? This kind of listening might be called "overlistening"—hearing more than was meant or just plain hearing a message that wasn't sent at all. For example, she says: "It would have been fun to have tried to make it as an industrial designer." He thinks: "She resents being a housewife and mother." Or, he says: "I really enjoy a simple dinner now and then." She thinks: "He didn't get enough to eat!"

Train yourself to be a good listener. It will improve your marriage, your friendships, in fact, all your relationships. As the Scriptures put it, all of us should "be quick to hear (a ready listener), slow to speak, slow to take offense and to get angry" (Jas. 1:19, *Amp.*).

Construction Is Harder than Destruction

In a marriage relationship most of us seem to come by the destructive skills—getting angry, being judgmental and critical, jealousy, pride, etc.—rather naturally. Building our mate up must be learned and it takes more than 10 easy lessons. For most marriage partners it's a lifetime course. Some never do too well. They often wind up in divorce court where they explain, "We are just destroying each other. It's better that we split up."

What is the secret? What does it take to build a marriage instead of tear it down? Some ideas that can help any marriage include the following:

Be understanding instead of always feeling "misunderstood." The world is overpopulated with people who are "misunderstood." Their wives are unreasonable. Their husbands are cruel. Their employers are tyrants. Their neighbors are out to get them. Their friends are heartless phonies.

And so it goes. We all know what it's like to feel misunderstood. As I talked with one group concerning this book, the ever-smiling Michelle confessed that she often felt misunderstood and then added rather wistfully, "But I'm a real nice person ... I'm really nice, you know?"

We all laughed with her, but I had to admit that I often say the same thing (usually under my breath of course). But what do we mean when we say, "Nobody understands me"? We may not want to face it but what we really mean is, "If only they were reasonable they would see that *I am right*. If they'll do it *my way*, everything will be fine!"

But for some strange reason these other people don't always want to do it "my way." They are unreasonable —even stubborn and unloving. So what can I do? The answer lies in a short prayer that is credited to Saint Francis of Assisi. It's a good prayer to repeat before going down to breakfast, before going to work, before getting home from shopping—anytime you are going to be talking and relating to others: "Lord! Grant that I may seek more to understand than be understood."

Or, as Paul wrote to the Christians at Ephesus: "Be patient with each other, making allowance for each other's faults because of your love" (Eph. 4:2, *TLB*).

We all have faults. To understand your spouse is not to say, "*Now*, I see your problem. You're just like your mother!" To understand is to say, "I see your point. I don't agree, but I accept you anyway."

Don't wait to be understood. It may never happen. Seek to understand and build a better marriage.[3]

Compliment instead of criticize. Being critical is one of our most natural destructive tendencies. To gripe and complain is as easy as breathing. It takes no brains, no training, no real talent. In marriage it's called nagging and it can turn a home into the opposite of heaven. Wives are supposed to be best at nagging:

"*When* are you going to fix the sink?"

"*Please* don't get anything messy!"

"You *never* take me anywhere."

Maybe that's why Solomon (with several hundred wives he should know) wrote: "A nagging wife annoys like constant dripping" (Prov. 19:13, *TLB*).

But husbands are really just as skilled at their own brand of nagging:

"*Why* don't you put more salt in the soup?"

"You mean my shirts aren't ironed—*again*?"

"When are we going to have a *hot* meal around here?"

Nagging, griping or complaining are sure marriage killers. As one unknown purveyor of marital wisdom said: "Often the difference between a successful marriage and a mediocre one consists of about three or four things a day left unsaid."

While criticizing is easy, paying compliments is usually more difficult. Most of us are awkward at paying an honest compliment in a sincere way. We are afraid the one we are complimenting won't believe us, or worse, he or she will think we are being phony. Another problem is that most people have a built-in resistance to compliments. Instead of accepting well-deserved praise, they think it is safer to "play it humble," or sometimes they really have a low self-image. Whatever the cause, they

134

can't enjoy being told that they look nice, that they do something well, etc.

So, between the hesitancy of the complimentors and the resistance of the complimentees, not many compliments get paid. Ironically, the compliment, one of the best tools for building a better marriage, gets rusty for lack of use!

If you think doing less criticizing and more complimenting is a worthwhile route to go, ask yourself these questions:

As I analyze my family relationships, do I see myself doing more complimenting or more criticizing?

Do I try to pay my spouse at least one sincere compliment each day?

Do I accept compliments gracefully or do I put my mate down by saying, "Oh, that's not really true," or, "Well, it was okay, but it could have been a lot better."

The song says "What the world needs now is love, sweet love." One way to start loving (caring for) your marriage partner is to cut the criticism and increase the compliments. As Solomon said, "A word spoken at the right moment, how good it is!" (Prov. 15:23, *AMP*).

Play up potential, play down pigeonholes. Have you ever felt that someone "never gave you a chance"? For example, as soon as your boss heard that you were a Democrat (German, Christian, or an exercise buff), he turned into an icicle. Or, perhaps you have been guilty of never-giving-someone-a-chance yourself. You hear, for example, that Mrs. Brown, your new neighbor, is a health food advocate so you vow you'll not have *her* over for coffee.

All of this is called pigeonholing—putting people in little slots where we think they fit. Another term for this is "labeling." We label people by their past, or by what we think we know about their past. It's easy to put people in pigeonholes or slap labels on them. It's kind of fun, too. It makes us feel superior, powerful and in control. Pigeonholing and labeling are often used in a marriage as a means of self-defense or as a subtle form of domination:

"When it comes to fixing things around here you can depend on Charlie to foul them up or not do them at all."

"That's my wife for you—*always* late."

There is another word for labeling or pigeonholing. It's called judging, something Jesus warned against in His Sermon on the Mount:

> *Do not judge lest you be judged [pigeon-holed] yourselves. For in the way you judge, you will be judged .... and why do you look at the speck in your brother's eye, but do not notice the log that is in your own eye? ... You hypocrites, first take the log out of your own eye; and then you will see clearly enough to take the speck out of your brother's eye* (Matt. 7:1-3,5).

It's so easy to see the "specks" in what others do, say and think. We forget the "logs" in our own behavior. Psychologists tell us that it's typical to judge certain faults in others because we have those same faults ourselves, but perhaps in a different form. By nailing our spouse, friends, fellow workers, etc., with their specks we hope to cover up our own logs.

For example, if we jump on our wives for always being late for appointments, is it because we always are late at work with handing in assignments? If we hit husbands with their inability to fix things well, are we trying to cover up our lack of skill or motivation to bake, sew, clean, etc. ?

But perhaps pigeonholing really isn't a problem for

136

WE LIMIT PEOPLE WITH LABELS

you. Be thankful and get to work on developing potential in the people you know fairly well. Seeing potential and giving it a chance to grow is what Christianity is all about. Even while we were sinners, God saw our potential. That's why He died for us. We are made right in God's sight by faith in His promises and we can have real peace with Him because of what Jesus did for us (see Rom. 5:1, *TLB*). God, the greatest finder and builder of potential of them all, has brought us to a special place. It's a place where we can "confidently and joyfully look forward to actually becoming all that God has had in mind for us to be" (Rom. 5:2, *TLB*).

God gave us a hand when we were helpless; He never labeled us "hopeless." As we relate to our marriage partner, can we do any less?

What Your Marriage Will Be, It Is Now Becoming

To paraphrase an old saying: What your marriage will be, it is now becoming.

Each of us brings to the altar exactly who we are and

no more. Then we have to put who we are with who "he" or "she" is. The result is marriage, which is: the most beautiful of relationships; the most difficult of relationships; the most basic of relationships.

Every marriage—from newlyweds to residents of the empty nest—can stand plenty of work. The Lord ordains marriage, but He needs your cooperation to sustain it. Pick any of the skills mentioned in this chapter and work at it. Or, do your *spouse* a favor, read a book on marriage and put it into action in your home.

And, in order to get God involved completely in sustaining your marriage, use one other skill that will make all the other techniques possible—prayer. Jesus tells us to ask and we will receive, to knock and the door will be opened to us, to seek and we will find (see Matt. 7:7). The ideal of lasting, happy marriage *is* reachable.

TO MAKE YOUR MARRIAGE GO,
CARE, COMMUNICATE, BE CONSTRUCTIVE.

HOW MUCH DO I VALUE MY FAMILY? PART VI

CHAPTER 18

IT'S a BIRD! IT'S a PLANE! IT'S SUPERPARENT!

The 1970s will go down as the decade of the superparent. Blissfully—and sometimes not so blissfully—unaware of the complicated process they had set in motion with the birth of junior, mom and dad were suddenly inundated by a bombardment of books, magazines, tapes, films and seminars on the fine art of parenting. A major target of all this family life lore was and still is the legendary communication gap between parents and children. From the kids' side come remarks like:

"They treat me like a baby."

"They don't trust me."

"They're always on my back."

"They're always comparing me to my brother (or sister)."

"They don't understand."

The list could go on and on and become very specific in regard to bedtimes, neatness, table manners, dating curfews, hairstyles, clothing, friends, money, etc., etc. The complaints vary according to the age of the child but the basic rub is always the child's will against the will of the parents.

And of course, from the parent's side come numerous comments about what drives *them* nuts:

"He won't clean up his room."

"She wants all freedom, no responsibility."

"He thinks money grows on trees."

"She wants to be trusted, but she does such crazy things!"

"They never show any appreciation, they think I'm the maid."

"They don't understand what it takes to keep a home going."

And so the charges fly back and forth as nobody on either side seems to "understand." Much has been made of the communication problem between today's children and their parents. The truth is, however, there has always been a communication problem between children and their parents, and there always will be.

A good way to approach the problem is to deal with it in the light of how much we really value our families, especially our children. What is your family—particularly your relationship with your children—worth to you? For many parents the answer is: "Everything. I love my kids!" For others, however, the reply might be: "Sometimes I'd sell them for a nickle." Or, "When does the next plane leave for Acapulco?"

Between these two extremes are a lot of people with mixed feelings. Sometimes their families are neat and other times they're nerve-racking. Without question, a good place to test our real values is right at home—with that lovable, laughable and sometimes ludicrous bunch called "my family."

Jesus didn't leave us His own short course in family living. But He did do and say several things that laid down principles for successful family life then—and now.

He Taught Respect and Honor for Parents

On one occasion the Pharisees came to Jesus with an honest (not tricky) question. They were genuinely puzzled as to why Jesus' disciples didn't go through all the elaborate rituals before eating, as they did. These rituals included a very special way of washing their hands before eating, holding their fingers and wrists just so. Strict Jews, in fact, would go through this washing ceremony, not only before each meal but between each of the courses![1]

As part of the answer to the Pharisees Jesus asked a rather loaded question of His own:

> *"Tell me," replied Jesus, "why do you break God's commandment through your tradition? For God said*, 'Honor thy father and thy mother,' *and* 'He that speaketh evil of father or mother, let him die the death.' *But you say that if a man tells his parents, 'Whatever use I might have been to you is now given to God,' then he owes no further duty to his parents. And so your tradition empties the commandment of God of all its meaning"* (Matt. 15:10, 11, *Phillips*).

Jesus accused the Pharisees of breaking God's commandments through their traditions because of their shameful practice of refusing to help their own parents who might be in dire need. Their excuse? Everything they had was *corban*—dedicated to God. The truth, of course, was that they used their money and possessions as they saw fit. If an elderly parent asked for help, they

142

would say, "Sorry, Dad, everything I have is officially dedicated to God and the Temple."

Jesus answered the Pharisees by exposing their hypocrisy to the clear light of day. They were neglecting a specific commandment of God (honor your father and mother) to obey a tradition of men that was not even in the Scriptures (the "law" of *corban*).[2] Their values had become so corrupt that they had things upside down. They had come to the place where their traditions and rituals meant more than the teachings of God's Word.

So there you have principle number one: "Honor your father and your mother"—and it's the only one of the Ten Commandments that also includes a promise—"that your days may be prolonged in the land which the Lord your God gives you" (see Exod. 20:12). This is an excellent principle, but without the balancing effect of other Scripture it can be misused. For example, some parents love to quote Exodus 20:12 as a blanket reason why children should *never* challenge parental reasoning (or lack of reasoning) on *any* subject. Fortunately, Jesus said and did other things that give us a more completely biblical picture.

Jesus Said Children Should Be Loved and Respected

In Matthew 19, we can find the following three short verses that tell us volumes about how Jesus saw the younger generation:

> Then some children were brought to Him so that He might lay His hands on them and pray; and the disciples rebuked them. But Jesus said, "Let the children alone, and do not hinder them from coming to Me; for the kingdom of heaven belongs to such as these." And after laying His hands on them, He departed from there (Matt. 19:13-15).

143

Imagine what this scene was like. Some mothers meet Jesus and His disciples and they try to bring their children to the Lord so He can touch and pray for them. These mothers have probably heard (or even seen) how Jesus heals people who are sick. Possibly some of the children are ill, or perhaps the mothers simply want Jesus to give them His special blessing.

The disciples represent the Don't-bother-me-kid-can't-you-see-we're-busy attitude that adults often show to young people. They aren't necessarily trying to be mean. They are just preoccupied with all that is going on. Jesus' days are filled with teaching, healing and helping people. Perhaps He is extra tired and late for His next appointment to boot. The disciples are simply trying to protect their Master from "unnecessary" interference.

But Jesus doesn't see the children as unnecessary bother. In so many words He says: "Don't try to stop the children from coming to me. In fact, everyone who comes to me should come with the same kind of faith and trust that these little ones have."

In this brief scene Jesus teaches a major principle about how adults are supposed to relate to the younger generation. From preschool to high school the principle Jesus teaches in this encounter is the same: adults should never brush somebody off because he or she is "just a kid."

What Jesus is teaching here is that *anyone can come to Him*, especially children. Jesus is saying that young people deserve the same respect and courtesy due adults, and that evens up the score concerning principles Jesus left us for happy family life. On one side we have the principle that children are to obey their parents. But on the other side we have the equally strong principle that parents are to treat their children fairly and respect

144

them as persons. It all sounds a great deal like the apostle Paul who told the Christians at Ephesus (Eph. 6:4, *TLB*):

AND NOW A WORD TO YOU PARENTS.
DON'T KEEP ON SCOLDING
AND NAGGING YOUR CHILDREN,
MAKING THEM ANGRY AND RESENTFUL.
RATHER, BRING THEM UP WITH LOVING DISCIPLINE
THE LORD HIMSELF APPROVES.

CHAPTER 19

THE PUZZLE OF PARENTING

Why is parenting such a puzzle? We don't start the day intending to criticize, preach, lecture, spank, humiliate, etc. No, we start with the prayer that we'll be loving, understanding, fair, just, reasonable, patient, etc. But before nightfall, or somewhere between sundown and the 10 o'clock news, it all comes apart. As child rearing specialist Haim Ginott succinctly puts it, "Once more we find ourselves saying things we do not mean, in a tone we do not like."[1]

And, if we are trying to rear our children "in the nurture and admonition of the Lord," we reap the additional burden of guilt when we fail to live up to the standards set in the Scriptures. Fortunately, the Lord is gracious and patient. And our kids are surprisingly resilient and forgiving as well. We can always hope to change for the better, *if we want to change.*

The following quizzes are designed to help you see

just how you value your children and certain aspects of your family relationships. Once you identify where you are in some of these areas, you can devise a plan of action for doing something about it.

Do You Trust and Respect Your Children?

When you are a parent it is easy to concentrate on worrying about how your children are behaving. Are they being good? Are they being sassy? Do they talk too much? Are they considerate? But every street has two sides. Following is a quiz to help you think about how your children would rate *you* regarding how you treat *them*. After each question write in the word that best describes you: *always, often, sometimes, never*. A scoring code appears below.

1. I treat my children with the same respect I do my adult friends and acquaintances _____
2. I trust my children _____
3. I am reasonable _____
4. I compliment my children _____
5. I try to see things as my children do _____
6. I am fair _____
7. I pray for my children _____

Scoring code—Score as follows: always, 4; often, 3; sometimes, 2; never, 1. If you scored over 20 your relationship to your children is excellent; between 15-19, your relationship is good; between 10-14, your relationship is fair, needs strengthening; below 10, you should probably send the kids to grandma's for awhile or get away alone with your spouse for a weekend.

Even if your children are unreasonable, irritable, etc., there is nothing keeping you from treating them better except your own pride and lack of sensitivity. Tune in to your children. Ask them how *they* would score you in the quiz above. If you can keep your temper, their answers could be most helpful.

How Judgmental and Critical Are You?

As the saying goes, if your children live with criticism, they will learn to be critical (of you as well as everyone else). Read each statement below. Check the comment that comes closest to what you would say to your child. A scoring code appears below.

1. When your child is slow, your usual reaction is:
_____ a. Good grief! You must be a cross between a snail and a turtle!
_____ b. Will you please hurry up? I'm in a big hurry.
_____ c. Take your time. We have a few minutes.

2. When your child is clumsy or inept you say:
_____ a. Well, what can I expect? You take after your father's side of the family.
_____ b. You clumsy ox! Won't you ever learn?
_____ c. Whoops! Everybody makes mistakes. Let's try it again.

3. Your child brings home a report card with two As, a B and two Cs. You comment:
_____ a. Two As and a B—now that's the way to go!
_____ b. Not too bad—if you could just turn those Cs into Bs.
_____ c. What's this with two Cs? You better pull those up in a hurry, young man!

4. Your daughter chooses a dress that is unbecoming. You say:
_____ a. The color doesn't do much for you at all. I'm surprised you picked it.

148

_____b. It's not my favorite color on you, but the sleeves are cut nicely.

_____c. What a terrible dress! I wish you had better taste.

5. Your son scores 16 points for his basketball team but they lose in the final seconds when he misses two free throws. Your analysis of the game:

_____a. Too bad you choked on those last two free throws.

_____b. Your shooting was okay, except for those free throws. Better work on those.

_____c. Sixteen points! And you got some key rebounds too.

Scoring code—A score is assigned to each possible answer. Check your answers against the scores below, then add up your total.

  1. (a) 2 (b) 4 (c) 6

  2. (a) 2 (b) 4 (c) 6

  3. (a) 6 (b) 4 (c) 2

  4. (a) 4 (b) 6 (c) 2

  5. (a) 2 (b) 4 (c) 6

A score of 25-30 says that you keep your critical remarks to a minimum; between 20-24 suggests that you are being more critical and judgmental than you possibly realize; from 15-19 says you are definitely on the critical side and should work to improve; below 15 suggests that you are a pretty hard parent to live with.

Do You Build Up or Tear Down?

It's amazing what our words do to a child's self-esteem. As chapters 9,10 and 11 pointed out, there is an epidemic of inferiority and poor self-image that attacks most families. Many esteem destroyers are outside the home, such as school, athletic teams, playmates. But a poor self-image can be learned at home as well.

The following quiz will give you some hints about how your children are experiencing you each day.

Check the answer that comes the closest to what you would say in each situation.

1. Your child hates to get up for school. Your typical approach is:

___a. It's hard to get up—take five more minutes and try it again.

___b. Yes, getting up is hard but you can't be lazy. Let's go.

___c. If you'd go to bed on time, you'd be able to get up, lazy bones.

2. Your child is about to leave for school and he has forgotten his lunch. You say:

___a. Hold it, you forgot your lunch again. You'd forget your head if it weren't attached.

___b. Here's your lunch. Have a good day.

___c. Try to remember your lunch, okay? It's a lot of work to pack it.

3. Your son is playing his stereo too loud—again. You say:

___a. Please turn that thing down. The neighbors will complain!

___b. Are you deaf or just retarded? Turn that junk off and leave it off!

___c. I'd really appreciate it if you could play your stereo a little softer. I can't handle it that loud.

4. Your child says something rude or "smart aleck." You reply:

___a. I don't appreciate that kind of language. Please stop it immediately.

___b. That kind of talk will get you into trouble if you're not careful.

___c. Your mouth is getting too big for your brain. Who do you think you are?

5. Your child complains about his new teacher at school. You comment:

____a. Oh come on now. Mrs. Smith is trying hard, I'm sure. You know you don't listen very well.

____b. Teachers have their moods. You'll just have to learn to get along.

____c. It sounds like Mrs. Smith is making life tough right now. You must be worried about what kind of grade you'll get.

Scoring code—A score is assigned to each possible answer. Check your answers against the scores given below, then add up your total.

1. (a) 6 (b) 4 (c) 2
2. (a) 2 (b) 6 (c) 4
3. (a) 4 (b) 2 (c) 6
4. (a) 6 (b) 4 (c) 2
5. (a) 2 (b) 4 (c) 6

A score of 25-30 means that you are an excellent builder of self-esteem in your children; between 20-24 suggests that you try to be positive but sometimes slip into using language that does little to build self-esteem; from 15-19 indicates that you may be helping to give your children a poor self-image; below 15 points to real problems—for your children's self-esteem and probably your own. The first book you should read is *Hide or Seek* by Dr. James Dobson.[2]

Quizzes Like This Give Only a Partial Picture

These three brief quizzes cannot possibly give you a complete picture of how you are relating to your children. They can only give you some hints about your basic attitudes and life-style. If you have several children, you may find that your answers differ in regard to each child. It's also possible that you may have a fairly high score but you are still uncomfortable in some of these areas. If so, go back over your answers and evaluate them closely. Of the three choices for each question, which statement comes the *closest* to how you might react. In answering quizzes like this it is easy to put down the answer that you would like to give rather than the answer that is closer to reality.

"I Want to Give Them the Right Values, But ... "

No question about it, parenting is a frustrating, even frightening, business. You have such hopes and dreams mixed with such fears and uncertainties. One mother of two elementary aged children put it well when she said: "I want to give them the right values, but I'm not always sure how to go about it."

Perhaps even more important than giving your children the "right values" is to *value them in the right way*. Instead of asking, "How can I be sure to teach my children correct values?" perhaps the more important question is "How much do I value my children? What can I do to let them know I cherish and prize them? How can I build them up as persons?"

No matter what your style of parenting is, the order for priority should be:

VALUE YOUR CHILDREN
THEN TEACH THE RIGHT VALUES.

CHAPTER 20

PRINCIPLES FOR PARENT POWER

Dozens of books and other products have been developed to help make you a better parent. They are filled with excellent advice, techniques and ideas. But some of the best principles for parenting have been in the Bible all along. The One who said, "Let the children come to me" taught many truths about how to value others in the highest kind of way. No Christian parent can go wrong if he uses the following principles as a basic foundation for any philosophy of child-rearing.

The Golden Rule Cuts Both Ways

Almost all parents want their children to respect, honor and obey them. They point to the fifth commandment[1] as proof of the mandate given to them by God Himself. But in Matthew 19, Jesus also taught respect and honor for children. When Jesus told His disciples that children had as much right to come to Him as anyone else, He was echoing His famous teaching:

"Treat others as you want them to treat you" (Luke 6:31, *TLB*).

Everybody agrees that the Golden Rule is a good idea— for the *other guy* to practice. Whatever the situation, we know exactly how others—especially our children—should treat *us*. It's harder, though, to think about how we should treat *them*.

There are many ways to practice the Golden Rule but one of the most practical approaches with your children is to show them as much respect as you expect from them. A good way to show respect for your children is through a communication technique called "active listening." When we use active listening we try to *hear* our child's feelings. When we actively listen we preserve our child's self-respect and make statements of understanding and empathy instead of handing out lectures and advice.[2]

Unfortunately, active listening is not widely practiced by parents. Instead, it is easier to respond to their questions and complaints with what some child-rearing specialists call the "Dirty Dozen":

1. *Ordering, directing, commanding:* "That's enough of *that*, young man!"

2. *Warning, admonishing, threatening:* "One more crack out of you and you've had it!"

3. *Exhorting, moralizing, preaching:* "Can't you see that talking that way is terrible?"

4. *Advising, giving solutions or suggestions:* "I don't think you should worry about it—why don't you just forget the whole thing?"

5. *Lectures, teaching, giving logical arguments:* "Jesus taught us to love one another. So that's what you should do, too."

6. *Judging, criticizing, disagreeing, blaming:* "You're always so impatient—won't you ever learn?"

7. *Praising, agreeing:* "Well, I'm sure an honest little girl like you can't be to blame."

8. *Name calling, ridiculing, shaming:* "Hey dummy, shut your big mouth!"

9. *Interpreting, analyzing, diagnosing:* "You've always had a problem getting along with Alice, haven't you?"

10. *Reassuring, sympathizing, consoling, supporting:* "Don't let it get you down. I remember how it was when I was in school."

11. *Probing, questioning, interrogating:* "Have you felt this way long about your sister?"

12. *Withdrawing, distracting, humoring, diverting:* "Don't bother me now. We can talk later."

Some specialists claim that 90 percent of all parental responses to their children fall into one of the above categories.[3] There are times, of course, when advising, teaching or suggesting are necessary. But they shouldn't always be the *first* thing you say. For example, suppose Mary comes home from her softball game, stomps in the door and practically screams, "We lost the game! The umpire called me out at the plate and everybody there said I was safe!" Any number of the dirty dozen responses might come to mind as a way of answering Mary:

"Don't use that tone of voice in this house."

"If you can't take it, don't play."

"Well that's the way it goes—all umpires make mistakes."

The parent who tries to practice active listening, however, would use one of these responses:

"My, sounds like you had a tough game!"

"Wow, you sure seem upset with that umpire."

"It must have been really frustrating to almost have the game won and then get called out."

With the above kind of responses you are reflecting the feelings of your child, trying to understand how it is with her. You give the child freedom to deal with her frustration, fear, anxiety, and try to share how she feels. Later, when the child has calmed down and is in a more receptive mood, it may be appropriate to make a suggestion or give some advice.

Active listening or listening for feelings is something all of us like to experience at any age. For example, suppose it's dinner time. Mom has worked hard all day. She gets home to find that the crockpot has quit working and dinner is only half cooked. As she tries to figure out how to salvage dinner, Jimmy, her nine-year-old, comes tearing in after skinning his knee in a fall from his bike. As she rummages for a Band-Aid, her husband walks in and the phone starts ringing in the other room. She says: "The crockpot conked out and dinner isn't done, Jimmy is hurt and now the phone!"

Which response from those below would be the most helpful for her husband to make?

"Good grief! Can't we get something dependable to cook with?"

"Well, how many times have I said Jimmy shouldn't be riding that bike on the hill?"

"Wow! Honey, it must be a drag to work all day and then come home to this. I'll patch Jimmy up, you get the phone and then we'll go out to eat."

Active listening—listening for feelings—sounds simple but it is not. Most of us are programmed by a lifetime of using the dirty dozen. In fact, we may even believe that it is our Christian duty to respond with advice, giving solutions or making "reasonable" suggestions and other seemingly positive statements, often in the form of Scripture verses. But as the above illustrations demonstrate, there are moments when all of us—child or adult—don't want advice or suggestions or even consolation. We want empathy—the feeling that the other person is trying to sense how it is to be in our shoes.

To learn more about the technique of active listening see the footnotes for this chapter. Don't expect to become a skilled active listener overnight. But the more you try to use this technique, the more the Golden Rule will be practiced at your house.

Put Down Your Guns

A lot of parents pride themselves in not allowing their children to even play with guns, yet these same parents may be guilty of firing away with a six-shooter of their own labeled "criticism." Jesus knew how much damage we can do with a critical tongue and that's why He said: "Don't criticize, and then you won't be criticized" (Matt. 7:1, *TLB*). Many Bible versions say "Judge not," but of course we all do. Passing judgment on others is a favorite sport we seem to learn at an early age (usually from our own parents!). And, when we get children of our own we continue in the same pattern. Being critical seems to be a necessary part of parenting:

"You're doing that all wrong."

"You're chewing with your mouth open again."

"You didn't tell us where you were going—that's very inconsiderate!"

Of course it's part of the parent's role to correct and train, but there is a difference between correction and criticism. When correction is necessary a good conversational strategy is to replace the "you message" (which usually heaps blame on the listener), with an "I message" (which simply shares personal feelings). It's so easy to get frustrated, exasperated, and downright angry with our children. We wind up sending "you messages" like machine-gun bullets:

a "YOU" message puts the other person on the defensive

an "I" message is less apt to do so

"You never think! You don't care! You're not trying! You're clumsy—always have been and always will be!"

When the word "you" is put on the front end of a message, the receiver of the message often gets defensive, particularly if that receiver is your child and the situation is tense or heated. Cure for the "you message" is the "I message." Far better to own your own feelings and share how you feel but with an "I" on the front of it, not a "you." For example, "I don't feel that is fair" is a lot less threatening to your child than "you're unfair" or "you have no consideration."

Instead of attacking your child with angry accusations, etc., it's better to admit you're angry by simply saying "I feel angry", or "Messes like this make me feel furious. I'd like to throw the whole thing right out the door."

Instead of getting on your son's case with, "You never put the tools away!" Better to say, "I really get frustrated when I can't find a screwdriver when I need it."

If you are interested in learning more about the advantage of using the "I message" instead of the "you message," see the suggested reading in the footnotes for this chapter. Keep in mind, however, that like active listening, learning to send "I messages" is not something you will do overnight. Like the dirty dozen, the "you message" is firmly programmed into our way of thinking and talking. But if we are interested in sounding less critical to our children in those moments when we have to direct them, the "I message" is a skill that is well worth developing.

Refuse to Retaliate

As Jesus put it: "Don't resist violence! If you are slapped on one cheek, turn the other too" (Matt. 5:39, *TLB*). This is not to suggest that you should allow your children to hit you or kick you in the shins while you say, "There, there, mother knows you're very angry." Discipline is a necessary part of rearing children. But when Jesus talks about turning the other cheek, what He is saying is to not take revenge, something that is all too easy to do in dealing with our children. We spank them out of revenge. We cut them down with sharp remarks out of revenge. They frustrate us, make us angry, disgusted and embarrassed and we often strike back to get revenge, whether we want to admit it or not.

How does a parent resist revenge? By being a relentless forgiver. Jesus had a great deal to say about forgiveness. One day Peter asked Him: " 'Sir, how often should I forgive a brother who sins against me? Seven times?'

" 'No!' Jesus replied, 'seventy times seven!' " (Matt. 18:21,22, *TLB*).

When Peter asked Jesus if forgiving seven times was enough, he thought he was being a good fellow indeed. The rabbis taught to forgive at least three times, so Peter felt extra spiritual by doubling this and adding one for good measure.[4] But Jesus wasn't interested in rationing forgiveness in exact amounts. That's why He said we should forgive *seventy times seven*. To forgive someone 490 times for something sounds a bit ridiculous and so it would be if you were really trying to keep score. But in families, especially, people shouldn't keep score on forgiving each other. When Jesus suggests forgiving someone 490 times He is saying we should forgive on an *unlimited basis*.

There is no better place to practice unlimited forgiveness than with your children:

Forgive when they spill the milk, drop the cup and break it, stumble and knock over the lamp.

Forgive when they get home late for supper, when they forget to pick up their clothes, when they are rude and thoughtless.

Forgive when you cross wills with your kids on wearing raincoats, dressing warm enough, and what time is reasonable for going to bed.

To be sure, practicing unlimited forgiveness does not mean practicing unlimited permissiveness. On many occasions children need correction and discipline, and to not give it is unloving and unbiblical. There are various styles of discipline (see suggested reading in the footnotes for this chapter) but any approach to discipline should be tempered by forgiveness. The ideal is to correct or discipline the *act* and still love the *child*, something that is not always easy when you are irritated, tired or just plain angry.

Conflicts are an inevitable part of living together in a family. Conflicts with children—major and minor—are routine in the day of any parent. To lash out and retaliate is human and easy; to forgive is Christian and a lot harder.

160

Active listening and the "I message" are useful tools, but they are no substitute for living within Christ's love. Jesus said: "When you obey me you are living in my love" (John 15:10, *TLB*). All techniques, skills and tools become only burdensome rules and legalistic quicksand without Christ's love at work in your life. Without your genuine concern, compassion and dedication to obeying the Lord's teachings, all techniques will fizzle or fail.

Communication is not just a two-way street; it's a three-way proposition. You have to be in communication with Christ in order to communicate correctly with your children.

For a review on communicating with Christ and feeling closer to Him, see chapter 4.

But You Don't Know What It's Like at My House!

Perhaps I don't—then again, perhaps I do. With a daughter in college and two sons in high school I know something about struggling with trying to practice the Golden Rule when other people don't "do unto me" as I would like. I have struggled with being an active listener; in fact my daughter Kim often assures me I'm not listening at all! I have worked with trying to send "I messages" to Jeff and Todd but too many of them still come out like "you messages."

As I said earlier in this chapter, none of these principles, skills or techniques are easy or simple. They all sound difficult and they *are* difficult. That's why people of all ages down through the centuries haven't been doing so well with them. It all comes back to a question of values. How much do I cherish and prize my children? Am I all wrapped up in being sure they know the "right values"? Or am I willing to keep trying to value them in a more supportive and helpful way?

If you are interested in being a better parent, the

resources available to you are practically unlimited. A brief list of some of the better books appears with the footnotes for this chapter.

Concentrate on one area at a time but always be working on something rather than rolling your eyes toward heaven and saying, "Lord, what *am* I gonna do with these kids?"

If anything is worth your time and tenacity, it's building a stronger family. And there is one good way to do that:

TRY TO VALUE YOUR CHILDREN AS MUCH
AS CHRIST VALUES THEM—AND YOU.

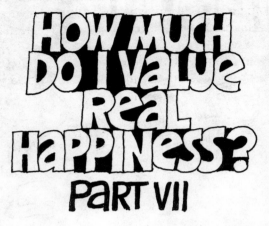

HOW MUCH DO I VALUE REAL HAPPINESS?

PART VII

CHAPTER 21

How can I live a Happy Life?

What does it take to be happy? A lot of people would like to know the answer to that one. We all value being happy. In fact, some people almost make a religion out of "pursuing happiness." The preachers of the happiness religion include:

TV pitchmen ("How's your love life?");

Real estate developers ("Get away to escape-country");

Politicians ("I promise cleaner air, lower taxes, higher wages, no oil spills").

But what about Christians? How does a Christian find happiness in this pressure cooker world? What is permissible and what is off limits? It is wrong for Christians to buy toothpaste that gets their teeth whiter? Cars that get better gas mileage? Homes that are in escape-country? It seems that this is where we came in with chapter 1. The world squeezes us gently but firmly as it claims that *this* is what we should value; *this* is what is worthwhile; *this* is the way to happiness!

Jesus said a great deal about how to be happy, but He would have had a tough time making it today in advertising, sales or politics. For example, picture Jesus as a copywriter for a big advertising agency in New York. He has turned in some copy on "Living the Good Life," and His boss, a hard-boiled copy editor, has responded with some comments of his own.

" *'Blessed [happy] are the poor in spirit, for theirs is the kingdom of heaven.'*

"Poor in spirit? Wait a minute, Jesus, what are you talking about? Everybody's reading books on how to look out for Number One—how to win through intimidation, how to assert yourself, how to succeed. Nobody gets hired if he doesn't have any spirit! That line would go a lot better like this: 'Happy are the confident, for they will always be able to handle anything!'

" *'Blessed [happy] are those who mourn, for they shall be comforted.'*

"C'mon, Jesus, you can't mean it. Mourning is a bummer. That's why we call cemeteries 'memorial parks' and why some people get buried in their Ferraris. We want to forget mourning, deny that death happened. Better to say, 'Happy are those who remember the good times and think positive thoughts!'

" *'Blessed [happy] are the meek, for they shall inherit the earth.'*

"Well, being meek and mild may be okay for a ladies' aid croquet match, but that's not where it's at in the real world. You've got to be tough to make it, to even survive. Some nice guys don't even finish last—they don't even finish! Better to put it like this: 'Happy are the gutsy who are willing to play for keeps, for they shall win more than they lose.'

" 'Blessed [happy] are those who hunger and thirst for righteousness, for they shall be satisfied.'

"Jesus, you've *got* to be kidding. Righteousness went out with Watergate, Hitler's gas ovens and Benedict Arnold. Hungering and thirsting for righteousness in *this* world is a waste of time. It's dog-eat-dog, cat, mouse, whatever comes your way. You've got to be on your toes or you'll wind up on somebody's trophy room wall. In this jungle we call 'life' it's 'Happy are the shrewd, for they are always a jump ahead of the other guy.'

" 'Blessed [happy] are the merciful, for they shall receive mercy.'

"Well, I'll admit that sounds pretty good, Jesus, but you've gotta be careful. Once you get someone on the ropes, better to let the old killer instinct take over. After all, he'll do the same to you if he can. Free enterprise isn't built on mercy, it's built on guts, hard work and the will to succeed. Everybody's got a sob story these days, but 'Happy are the hardnosed for they won't be played for a sucker.'

" 'Blessed [happy] are the pure in heart, for they shall see God.'

"Here we go again, back to that goody-two-shoes stuff. *Nobody's* pure in heart, Jesus. Didn't you say yourself that you came to bring all us sinners to repentance? To be pure in heart means you've got to trust people and where does *that* get you? Just ask John F. Kennedy, Abraham Lincoln, or Julius Caesar. Come to think of it, you didn't do too well trusting Judas, did you? It's a lot more realistic to say: 'Happy are those who never trust anyone, for they shall seldom be disappointed.'

" 'Blessed [happy] are the peacemakers, for they shall be called sons of God.'

166

"Sounds interesting, Jesus. But what we need in this world is men with conviction, men who will stand up on their hind legs and be counted. Nobody likes war but sometimes it's better than peace at any price, because the price can be too high. Today it makes more sense to say: 'Happy are those who stick to their guns and stand up for their rights for they won't get pushed around.' "

The hard-boiled copy editor sounds like he's been around the track a few times. Not exactly the type you would want for your dentist, but definitely realistic and wise to the ways of today's world. But does he have the real picture of what Jesus is saying? Let's look again at these brief sentences by Jesus that are called "The Beatitudes"—descriptions of supreme happiness.

Blessed Are the Poor in Spirit (Matt. 5:3)

At first glance we can understand why the copy editor isn't too turned on by "poor in spirit." He pictures someone with no pep, no zest for life, no *gusto!* But that isn't what Jesus means at all. Nor does He mean we should lack courage or the will to succeed.

What "poor in spirit" does mean is: "Be humble, willing to admit that God is very great and you are very small." Isaiah was poor in spirit when he said: "Woe is me . . . because I am a man of unclean lips" (Isa. 6:5). King David was poor in spirit when he said, "Who am I, O Lord God . . . that Thou hast brought me this far? " (2 Sam. 7:18). Peter was poor in spirit when he said to Jesus: "Depart from me, for I am a sinful man, O Lord" (Luke 5:8).

For the Christian, to be poor in spirit means having the genuine awe and humility that come from knowing that you need God. To realize this takes off all the pressure. You don't have to make it on your own. You don't have to produce your own self-esteem. You trust

God for everything and His strength is there to draw upon. To do a little rewriting on the copy editor's cynical views: "Happy are those who know how much they need God and who are not too proud to admit it, for they will enjoy doing God's will."

Blessed Are They That Mourn (Matt. 5:4)

Our editor friend was right when he said people do all they can to escape mourning and sadness. After all, there is too much misery in the world already; why make it sound like fun by suggesting that someone who is mourning can be happy?

But again the editor missed Jesus' meaning. The Lord isn't saying, "Now that your entire family has been wiped out by a tornado you can really celebrate!" When a loved one or close friend dies or is in serious danger we are sad, and rightfully so.

So what is Jesus saying? He is speaking in spiritual terms. For the Christian to "mourn" in a spiritual sense means to *really care*, way down deep inside, about your relationship to Christ. This second beatitude flows naturally out of the first.[1] As we become "poor in spirit" we see God's greatness and holiness and have to admit our helplessness without Him. In a word, we have to admit our sin, that we miss the mark and fall short of God's glory. This has to make us feel sorry, regretful.

But how can feeling sad make us happy? Because it doesn't stop there. To feel sorry is to repent, a solid biblical word that isn't used so much these days. It sounds too old-fashioned, maybe "too religious." Instead, we toss God a "Sorry about that, Lord," and try to think of happier things. But to repent is to be sorry and really mean it. Repenting is not much fun but it is the way to real happiness. When we admit our sin to God, He helps us. He forgives us and we are comforted.

168

To put it in language the copy editor might better understand: "Happy is the Christian whose sin makes him miserable until he confesses it to God and is forgiven."

Blessed Are the Meek (Matt. 5:5)

Hardboiled advertising copy editors always have a tough time with the idea of being meek. One of the modern definitions of meek is "spineless, easily imposed upon." Spineless people don't inherit the earth; they're lucky to get that cheap vase left to them by Aunt Martha. There are other definitions of meek, however, including: mild of temper, patient under injury, gentle and kind. And this is what Jesus has in mind. It takes plenty of backbone to be gentle, kind and patient, especially when the heat is on.

Biblically speaking, the meek person is under control. He has self control—actually Christ-control.[2] Christ provides the strength to handle frustration, unfairness, criticism and all the other problems that come our way each day.

The hardened copy editor may not agree, but according to Jesus, "Happy are the nice guys who keep their

HAPPY ARE THE NICE GUYS FOR THEY DO FINISH FIRST— SOMETIMES

MOST UNSELF-ISH

cool and are controlled by Christ, because they will have their share of finishing first."

Blessed Are They Which Do Hunger and Thirst After Righteousness (Matt. 5:6)

You can't blame our copy editor for being cynical about this one. To him, righteousness means morality, doing the right thing. Moral righteousness seems in short supply in a world full of dope pushers, terrorists, con artists, cheaters on income tax and hypocrites of all kinds, especially the kind he believes are in the church.

The Bible is certainly for morality and doing what is right, but this isn't the kind of righteousness to which Jesus is referring in this fourth beatitude. Part of the biblical meaning of righteousness is: to be justified, declared righteous in God's sight because you believe in Christ as Saviour from sin. But Jesus has even more in mind. He's thinking of another theological mouthful—sanctification. To be sanctified means to be set apart for God and to grow more and more like Christ.

In a few words, then, to hunger and thirst for righteousness means to really want to let Christ control your life. As He takes control, being moral and doing the right thing takes care of itself.

But notice that Jesus says we should *hunger and thirst* for the righteousness He gives. When you are really hungry or thirsty, you want food and water in the worst way. You're desperate for something to eat or drink. To put it in terms the copy editor might better understand: "Happy is the Christian who is starving to know Christ better for he will have a banquet indeed!"

Blessed Are the Merciful (Matt. 5:7)

It's not too hard to understand why the copy editor is skeptical about showing mercy. It *is* a dog-eat-dog world as far as he's concerned. Practically from the cradle we are taught to compete, to outdo the other guy in the classroom, in sports, in business, in all walks of life. Nevertheless, what Jesus says about our caring enough to show mercy should make good sense to us all. We are far more likely to receive mercy if we show it to others. In many places of the New Testament, we are warned against not showing mercy or not granting forgiveness. (See for example, the Parable of the Unmerciful Servant in Matt. 18:23-35.)

The biblical word for mercy goes all the way back to a Hebrew expression that refers to the ability to get inside the other person's skin, to see with his eyes, to think with his thoughts, feel as he feels.[3] Today we call this *empathy*. No one ever showed more empathy than God Himself. He had mercy on us while we were helpless sinners. He sent His son to be our Saviour. And Christ understood our problem, "Since he had the same temptations we do, though he never once gave way to them and sinned" (Heb. 4:15, *TLB*).

The Christian is someone who knows he is forgiven through God's grace and mercy. The Christian "knows how it is" for the other person. He can forgive and show mercy because he has been forgiven.[4] To help the skeptical copy editor understand, this beatitude might be paraphrased to say: "Happy is the Christian! He can show mercy because he knows that in the final outcome God will show him mercy!"

Blessed Are the Pure in Heart (Matt. 5:8)

We can easily see why our pessimistic copy editor says no one is pure in heart. He is right, because everyone is a sinner and if all we had to go on was our own human "goodness" our situation would be completely hopeless.

So what does Jesus mean? What is a pure heart and how do you get one?

First, understand that a person's "heart" is not the muscle that pumps blood. Biblically speaking, your heart is the center of your being. It involves your brain, your mind, your will, your soul. Your heart is the total you.[5]

Second, to be pure in heart means to cut the hypocrisy. It means having a single purpose and direction, not being double-minded and unstable (see Jas. 1:8). Today's jargon includes phrases like "getting your act together," "putting it all together" and "being together." The psalmist prayed and asked God to "unite my heart to fear Thy name" (Ps. 86:11). In other words he was asking God to help him get it together. He wanted to center his life on the Lord.

Third, pureness of heart certainly suggests being clean. David prayed, "Create in me a clean heart, O God" (Ps. 51:10). At the time he really needed one. The prophet Nathan had just nailed him about his sin of adultery with Bathsheba and the murder of her husband, Uriah. There is no way to cleanse your own heart. Only the Holy Spirit can do it. That's why David also prayed "Take not thy Holy Spirit from me" (Ps. 51:11, *KJV*).

Fourth, if we are pure in heart we shall see God. We don't deserve to see God, but we will if we let Christ help us put our lives in order.

To help our copy editor friend be a little more optimistic, the sixth beatitude could be put in these terms: "Happy is the Christian whose life is together and centered on Christ, for he will know that God is very close."

Blessed Are the Peacemakers (Matt. 5:9)

A man of the world, such as our copy editor friend, is caught in a dilemma when it comes to peace. He wants

172

world peace all right and he hopes the diplomats can keep everybody's trigger finger off the H-Bomb buttons. But on a personal basis, things are different. He wants to stick up for his rights, not get walked on. He wants to stand for his convictions.

But, "standing for convictions and rights" is often done selfishly or greedily. As James says: "What causes fights and quarrels among you? Don't they come from your desires that battle within you?" (Jas. 4:1, *NIV*). Jesus says we will be happier if we strive to make peace. As the old saying puts it, "The way of the peacemaker is hard," but to be a warmaker is easy. A little dig here, a little chop there and you can have the place in an uproar, all the while acting under the guise of "only protecting my rights!"

To strive for peace, however, means more than just being passive, just being a good guy who "won't make a big thing out of it." Peacemaking also involves actively going out of your way to make things right.

Remember, it takes more power to make peace than it does to make war. The truly powerful person is usually the meek and gentle person who chooses his words carefully. The truly powerful person doesn't have to yell and scream to get people to listen.

Who are the peacemakers at your house? Where you work? It takes two to make war, only one to make peace.

That copy editor who wants to stand up for his rights might better understand Jesus if the seventh beatitude was put like this: "Happy is the Christian who makes peace not by giving in, but by giving himself to others. For he will be recognized as one of God's family."

Happiness Is Not for Sale

No, Jesus wouldn't have made it working for the worldly-wise copy editor, but then the copy editor's attitude toward life wouldn't get him a front row seat in the Kingdom of God either. It seems to be a question of values. In these seven beatitudes (we'll talk about the other two in chapter 23) the Lord turns the world's value system right on its ear. Happiness isn't something you can buy, sell, find or manufacture. Happiness, says Jesus, lies in first being aware of your real needs—admitting you are poor in spirit, feeling truly sorry (mourning) because of your sin and becoming meek (gentle) because you realize how self-centered you really are. The answer to these needs is to hunger and thirst for righteousness and then you will be filled with God's strength and power. And as a result of being filled you become merciful, pure in heart and a peacemaker. This isn't an easy route to happiness, but it's the way Jesus is headed. And in the Beatitudes Jesus asks every Christian, "Going my way?"

HAPPY ARE THOSE WHO:
- KNOW THEY NEED GOD
- ARE MISERABLE WHEN THEY SIN
- ARE CONTROLLED BY CHRIST
- ARE STARVING TO KNOW HIM BETTER
- KNOW MERCY AND SHOW MERCY
- CENTER THEIR LIVES ON CHRIST
- MAKE PEACE, NOT WAR

FOR THE GOOD LIFE SHALL BE THEIRS.

CHAPTER 22

SCALING THE BEATITUDES

No question about it, the Beatitudes are awesome. They rise out of the Bible like a 25,000-foot Himalayan mountain range—jagged peaks of perfection that soar hopelessly out of our reach.

One thing keeps us from giving up. When Jesus taught the Beatitudes He gave us goals to shoot at, not states of perfection we must achieve overnight or else. How much the Beatitudes become part of our experience and how happy we are as we incorporate them into our lives depends on our values, which are always under construction. The following "Beatitudes Inventory" gives you a workable way to see how well you are adapting Jesus' plan for happiness.

After each statement put in the number that matches the word best describing your attitude or actions at the present time. 1. Never; 2, Rarely; 3, Occasionally; 4, Sometimes; 5, Frequently; 6, Usually; 7, Always.

Happy are the poor in spirit
1. I think about how helpless I am without God ____
2. God is at the center of my life ____
3. Others consider me a humble person ____

Happy are those who mourn
1. I get very upset when I sin ____
2. Repentance is part of my life ____
3. When I sin my attitude is "Sorry about that, Lord" ____

Happy are the meek (gentle)
1. People consider me a meek person ____
2. I lose my temper ____
3. I try to be patient ____

Happy are those who hunger and thirst for righteousness
1. I am growing in Christ ____
2. I act like a hypocrite ____
3. I feel I am right with God ____

Happy are the merciful
1. I am very competitive ____
2. I have the killer instinct ____
3. I can put myself in the other person's shoes ____

Happy are the pure in heart
1. Jesus helps me "get it together" ____
2. Serving Christ is what I want to do ____
3. My life needs straightening out ____

Happy are the peacemakers
1. I am known for standing up for my rights ____
2. I make no trouble for anyone ____
3. I make an effort to make peace ____

Now go back over your answers. Sometimes you may have answered somewhere between 1 and 4 when you know it should have been somewhere between 5 and 7. Sometimes the better answer would have been between 5 and 7 and you may have been down between 1 and 4. It depends on how the question is worded. The purpose of this Beatitudes Inventory is to help you identify just where you stand in regard to what Jesus taught and how important these teachings should be in your life. Which beatitudes do you want to work on? How do you intend to go about it?

It's probably better to say you don't work on the Beatitudes, you let the Beatitudes work on you. More correctly, you let Christ work in your life. Scripture tells us God is at work in us "to will and to work for His good pleasure" (Phil. 2:13), but He doesn't make many changes without our permission or cooperation. Sometimes God picks us up by the "scruff of the neck," so to speak, and gives us a good shake, but usually His method is to work slowly according to how much we are willing to let Him change us.

Jesus gave us the Beatitudes to help us see where we are and how far we have to grow. The Beatitudes are not just for a special few who qualify to wear the title "Super Spiritual." *The Beatitudes are for every Christian.* And the more a Christian is like this, the happier and more worthwhile his or her life will be.

LET THE BEATITUDES CHANGE YOU
NO MATTER HOW LONG IT TAKES.

CHAPTER 23

The questions we are trying to answer in these final chapters are:

How can I be sure my life will be worthwhile?

How can I live a happy life?

With the Beatitudes in the background to draw from as we need them, let's try to answer these two giant questions by asking two smaller ones:

What is my purpose?

What are my goals?

What Is My Major Purpose in Life?

When trying to identify something as big as "my major purpose in life" it helps to understand that a purpose is not the same as a goal. Goals are specific objectives, such as getting a raise by the end of the year or learning to speak Spanish by April. Purposes, however, are broader and more general.[1] A purpose can be a guiding principle for actions toward others, such as, "to bring happiness to everyone I can." A purpose could also incorporate a quality of character you want to develop, such as "being a loving person" or "being a good listener."

Without a worthy purpose our lives have no real meaning. Without meaning and purpose, some people can literally give up and die.

Dr. Victor Frankl, a psychologist known throughout the world for his work in Logotherapy, was imprisoned in Nazi concentration camps during World War II. Day after day he and his fellow prisoners watched as some of their number were chosen to go to the gas chambers and then to cremation in the ovens. They watched their bodies wither away due to semi-starvation as they put in hard labor on 10½ ounces of bread and 1¾ pints of thin soup per day. They lived in freezing cold with no heat and only rags for clothing. Their feet swelled so badly with edema they could barely march to work. Their shoes, left unlaced because of the swelling, filled with snow and ice and every step was torture.

Frankl and the other prisoners became so weak they could not climb the two six-inch steps back into their prison barracks each night without stopping to grasp the door jamb with their hands and pull themselves through it.

In these hopeless conditions many men lost hope. Once without faith in their own future, they were doomed. It usually happened suddenly—a prisoner refusing to get up and report to the parade grounds for work detail. Pleas, threats and blows would not move him. He simply gave up and lay there in his own filth until he died or was executed.

The prisoners who somehow survived the horrors of concentration camps like Auschwitz were those who held on to hope and meaning for their lives by the slenderest of threads. Somehow, someday they hoped to get back to their families. Somehow, someday their suffering would be worth it. Those who believed in God usually found extra strength for their ordeal. As long as a prisoner could see some "why" for his terrible existence, he was able to bear almost any "how."[2]

For most of us, identifying completely with prisoners in a Nazi death camp is not easy. As we watched the horrors of Auschwitz, and Treblinka reenacted in the TV docu-drama, "Holocaust," it was difficult to imagine something that horrible happening to us. It was all so far away, so long ago.[3]

Still, Dr. Frankl's experience focuses the tremendous importance of having purpose and meaning in life. What should be your major purpose in life? If you ask this kind of question in a Sunday School class or your neighborhood Bible study, you will probably get answers like: "to glorify God," "to be a dedicated disciple," "to serve Christ." All of these are excellent purposes—broad objectives that we would like to reach, although we don't always know quite how to go about it.

What's the answer to having your purpose as a Christian clearly in focus and *keeping it that way*? Jesus puts it all into much sharper perspective when He tells us that *hungering and thirsting after righteousness* is the way to be filled. Call it "growing in Christ," "becoming more like Jesus," or "Christian maturity," it all adds up to a genuine desire to let God work in your life.

In checking your purpose as a Christian, ask, "Where am I going? What does God want to do through me?"

What Are My Goals?

When you set goals you get down to specifics. A goal is something you can measure, something you can look back on and say, "I made it!" or "Better luck next time."

180

Goals can be rather minor things and very short range. For example, some of the goals one person might have for just one day could be:

- Catch the 8:10 bus for work.
- Return the books I borrowed from the library.
- Eat lunch with Bill and Marge.
- Do the marketing on the way home.
- Call my sister and invite her and her family for dinner on Saturday.

Longer range goals could be set for anywhere from several days and weeks to several months in advance. For example:

- Take a refresher course in shorthand this fall.
- Get promoted to division manager by spring.
- Read five books by the end of the year.
- Start a Bible study at work by the end of the month.
- Finish sewing a new dress by next week.

It's easy to see that our lives can be filled with all kinds of goals. Some are forced on us by others—employers and family for example—but we must choose a lot of goals for ourselves. A look at our goals tells us quickly how we are using our time and how we see life. It will also give us some good indicators concerning how happy we are, how worthwhile we think life is right now. Set no goals of your own and you will drift through life letting children, spouse, friends, employers, etc., set all your goals for you. It's a sign of maturity when a person starts setting his own goals and doing something to reach them.

A Beatitudes Experiment

According to Jesus, we will be blessed (happy) as the Beatitudes become part of our own experience. Here is one way to take specific action to make the Beatitudes happen in your life:

Step One: Make a special promise to Christ.

Step Two: Write that promise down.

Step Three: Keep that promise by doing it for 10 days in a row.

Your promise may involve doing something that is quite difficult or you may choose something simpler, not quite so heaven-shaking in scope. Whatever you promise, just be sure it takes you in the direction you want to go (the same way Christ is traveling) and that you will be sure to carry it out for 10 days.

As you probably have already guessed, making a promise is the same thing as setting a goal. See what kinds of goals you can come up with that are related to developing humility, genuine repentance of sin, meekness and gentleness, a hunger and thirst for righteousness, a merciful spirit, purity of heart, or the ability to be a peacemaker. Some starter ideas include:

Pray daily asking God to make you more sensitive to sin and being sorry when you slip up.

Read a chapter in the book of Proverbs each day and write down one thing you learn.

Work on being meek (Christ-controlled) while talking with your spouse, children, friends, work associates, etc. (Even if you blow it and lose your temper, the goal is to consciously *try*.)

Pick a different beatitude each day and paraphrase it (write it down in your own words).

Develop greater humility by doing something each day that combats false pride. Examples: admit you were wrong, say you're sorry, or go out of your way to help and serve someone.

Develop a greater sensitivity to sin by looking back on each day and confessing to God your sins of the tongue —unkind remarks, gossip, anger, etc.

Whatever promise you make, it is vital that you keep

it. A promise kept is a powerful weapon that gives you more confidence, more power to grow in your Christian walk. But a promise broken will erode your confidence and discourage you. If you do happen to fail in your 10-day commitment, *don't give up.* Confess it, forget about it, and *try again.*

Blessed Are the Persecuted?

No question about it, a Christian should never run out of specific goals to help him or her grow spiritually. God gives each of us the responsibility to set spiritual goals. And as you set these spiritual goals and start to reach them, don't be surprised if the eighth and ninth beatitudes become part of your life as well:

> *Blessed are those who have been persecuted for the sake of righteousness, for theirs is the kingdom of heaven.*
> *Blessed are you when men revile you, and persecute you, and say all kinds of evil against you falsely, on account of Me"* (Matt. 5:10, 11).

The early Christians went through incredible and horrible persecution: torn to bits by lions and wild dogs; burned at the stake and made into torches to light Nero's gardens. In less severe cases they would be fired from their jobs or lose all the customers from their trade or business.

Today, most Western Christians are not persecuted in such drastic ways. But living for Christ can still run you smack into the world's value system and when that happens you can expect misunderstanding, anger, mockery, division, and snide remarks. Why, then, does Jesus say the Christian who is persecuted will be happy? Because he or she will be living according to Christ's value system, not the world's. A good way to test just how com-

a PURPOSE as BROAD as
"TO GROW as a CHRISTIAN
as I GLORIFY GOD"
CAN INCLUDE MANY MORE
GOALS THAN THE THREE
SAMPLES aBOVE.
WHAT PERSONAL GOALS
WOULD YOU LIST
HERE?

mitted you really are to Christ is to ask yourself:

"What is Jesus worth to me? How much am I willing to take (or give up) for His sake?"

What Is a Happy Worthwhile Life?

The complete answer to that one may take many years to discover, but you have two good clues if you can say:

My life purpose is to grow in Christ—to let God work in my life as I glorify Him.

I am setting and reaching spiritual goals through Him.

The world has much to offer and it is often hard to decide what is really important. But the crucial key is to put Christ first and let everything else follow as He directs. Jesus said as much when He told His disciples:

> *If anyone wants to follow in my footsteps he must give up all right to himself, take up his cross and follow me. For the man who wants to save his life will lose it; but the man who loses his life for my sake will find it. For what good is it for a man to gain the whole world at the price of his own soul? What could a man offer to buy back his soul once he had lost it?* (Matt. 16:24-26, *Phillips*).

That is Jesus' final word on values. It is our final word also.

HAPPY IS THE CHRISTIAN
WHO VALUES CHRIST ABOVE ALL
FOR HE WILL ALWAYS KNOW
WHAT IS REALLY IMPORTANT
AND HE WILL NEVER GIVE UP
THE THINGS THAT ARE.

Notes

Notes for Introduction
1. See Sidney Simon, *Meeting Yourself Half-Way* (Niles, IL: Argus Communications, 1974), pp. viii-xi.
2. See for example Louis E. Raths, Merril Harmin, Sidney B. Simon, *Values and Teaching* (Columbus, OH: Charles E. Merril Publishers, 1966); Sidney B. Simon, J. Clark, *More Values Clarification* (San Diego, CA: Pennant Press, 1975); Howard Kirschenbaum, Sidney B. Simon, eds., *Readings in Values Clarification* (Minneapolis, MN: Winston Press, 1973).
3. See John 1:1-18; Hebrews 4:12; Psalm 119:89; Isaiah 40:8; 1 Peter 1:23-25; Colossians 3:16.
4. Cathleen Decker, "Vendor Shot, Bystanders Loot His Ice Cream Truck," *Los Angeles Times*, February 22, 1973, Part I, p. 3.

Notes for Chapter 1
1. For an insightful and sometimes inciting view of how worldly pressures are affecting Christians see *The Worldly Evangelicals* by Richard Quebedeaux (San Francisco: Harper and Row, 1978). Two stimulating periodicals dedicated to helping Christians evaluate and question their life-style are: *The Other Side*, Box 158, Savannah, Ohio 44874. *Sojourners*, 1029 Vermont Ave. NW, Washington, DC 20005.
2. Dwight Whitney, "What Uproar Over Soap?" *TV Guide* (November 26-December 2, 1977), p. 4.
3. Cecil Smith, "James at 16: Loss of Innocence," *Los Angeles Times*, February 9, 1978, Part IV, p. 1. Smith, by the way, is the same critic who called "Soap" a prolonged dirty joke. Without absolute standards from the Scriptures, a secular opinion can vary according to personal taste.
4. D. Martyn Lloyd-Jones, *Studies in the Sermon on the Mount* (Grand Rapids: Wm. B. Eerdmans Publishing Co., 1959), p. 79ff.
5. William Barclay, *The Gospel of Matthew*, The Daily Study Bible (Edinburgh: The Saint Andrew Press, 1956), vol. 1, pp. 241,242.
6. *Los Angeles Times*, November 29, 1977.
7. Barclay, *Matthew*, vol. 1, p. 244.
8. Barclay, *Matthew*, vol. 1, p. 244.
9. Harvey Cox, *Turning East: The Promise and Peril of the New Orientalism* (New York: Simon & Schuster, 1977).

Notes for Chapter 3
1. "Emperor Crowns Himself in Poverty-Stricken Land," *Los Angeles Times*, December 5, 1977, p. 1.

2. Reported on the NBC television program, "Weekend," January 7, 1978.

3. David and Beatrice Alexander, eds., *Eerdman's Handbook of the Bible* (Grand Rapids: Wm. B. Eerdmans Publishing Co., 1973), p. 484.

4. See also Everett F. Harrison, ed., *Baker's Dictionary of Theology* (Grand Rapids: Baker Book House, 1960), pp. 461,462.

5. Merrill F. Unger, *Unger's Bible Dictionary* (Chicago: Moody Press, 1957), p. 927.

6. D. Martyn Lloyd-Jones, *Studies in the Sermon on the Mount* (Grand Rapids: Eerdmans Publishing Co., 1959), vol. 2, p. 143.

Notes for Chapter 4

1. Among the many proverbs that could apply are: being popular—15:1; 17:7; being successful—3:5,6; 16:3; being good at what you do—6:6-11.

2. See especially Jesus' words in John 15:10-14; Luke 6:30-38; Mark 12:28-31. Also see Ephesians 4:32; Philippians 1:9-11; Colossians 3:12-17; Romans 12:9,10 for just a few key examples of one of the major themes in the New Testament: loving kindness.

Notes for Chapter 5

1. See John 14:26; 15:26; 16:7-14.

2. Attributed to Harvey Cox, Ph.D., Chairman of the Department of Applied Theology, Harvard Divinity School. Professor Cox is the author of several books.

Notes for Chapter 6

1. Adapted from *Decisions and Outcomes*, H.B. Gelatt, Barbara Varenhorst, Richard Carey, Gordon P. Miller (New York: College Entrance Examination Board, 1973), pp. 6,7.

Notes for Chapter 7

1. Charles F. Pfeiffer and Everett F. Harrison, eds., *The Wycliffe Bible Commentary* (Chicago: Moody Press, 1962), p. 1104.

2. William Barclay, *The Gospel of John*, The Daily Study Bible (Edinburgh: The Saint Andrew Press, 1965), vol. 2, p. 183.

3. Francis Thompson, "Ex ore Infantum."

4. See especially chapter 2, Alexander I. Solzhenitsyn, *The Gulag Archipelago* (New York: Harper and Row, Publisher, Inc., 1973).

5. "Would You Kill Idi Amin?" *Campus Life* (December, 1977), p. 57.

Notes for Chapter 8

1. For other references on Jesus' deity see John 10:30; John 12:45; John 1:1; Matthew 3:17; Matthew 12:18.

2. Brother Lawrence, *The Practice of the Presence of God* (Old Tappan, NJ: Fleming H. Revell Co., 1895), p. 8.

3. Lawrence, p. 10.

4. Lawrence, p. 32.

5. Lawrence, p. 34.

6. Lawrence, p. 35.

7. Lawrence, p. 44.

Notes for Chapter 9

1. Ralph Keyes, *Is There Life After High School?* (Boston: Little, Brown & Co., 1976), p. 16.

2. Keyes, *Is There Life After High School?*, p. 16

3. Keyes, *Is There Life After High School?*, pp. 16-18.

4. Robert H. Schuller, *Self-Love: The Dynamic Force of Success* (Old Tappan, NJ: Spire Books, 1975), pp. 15-22.

5. John Piper, "Is Self-Love Biblical?" *Christianity Today* (August 12, 1977), pp. 6-9.

6. William Barclay, *The Gospel of Matthew*, The Daily Study Bible (Edinburgh: The Saint Andrew Press, 1956), vol. 1, p. 401.

Notes for Chapter 10
1. James Dobson, *Hide or Seek* (Old Tappan, NJ: Fleming H. Revell Co., 1974), chaps. 1-3.
2. Charles M. Schulz, "Peanuts," United Features Syndicate, Inc., February 24, 1978.
3. George Sanchez, "The Scriptural Context for Realistic Self-Esteem," *Navlog* (January, 1978), p. 12.
4. John R.W. Stott, "Must I Really Love Myself?" *Christianity Today* (May 5, 1978), pp. 34,35. In an attempt to clarify the meaning of "self-love" from a biblical perspective, Stott says that we should always work within a theological framework that sees us as the product of the Fall on one hand, and the creation of God and recreation of Christ on the other hand. Having this balanced view of our self-image "will lead us beyond self-acceptance to something better still, namely self-affirmation. We need to learn both to affirm all the good within us, which is due to God's creating and recreating grace, and ruthlessly to deny (i.e., repudiate) all the evil within us, which is due to our fallenness."

Notes for Chapter 11
1. Ken Olson, *The Art of Hanging Loose in an Uptight World* (New York: Fawcett Crest Books, 1974), pp. 19-21.
2. Olson, *The Art of Hanging Loose*, chaps. 2–4.
3. Olson, *The Art of Hanging Loose*, chap. 5.
4. Gail Magruder, *A Gift of Love* (Philadelphia: A.J. Holman Co., 1976), p. 59.
5. William Barclay, *The Letters to Philippians, Colossians and Thessalonians*, The Daily Study Bible (Edinburgh: The Saint Andrew Press, 1959), p. 99.
6. Barclay, *Philippians, Colossians and Thessalonians*, p. 99.
7. Other secular books dealing with self-esteem, to which you can apply biblical principles include: Mildred Newman and Bernard Berkowitz with Jean Owen, *How to Be Your Own Best Friend* (Chicago: Valentine Books, 1974). Jess Lair, *I Ain't Much Baby, but I'm All I've Got* (New York: Fawcett Crest Books, 1972).
   Good books on self-esteem written from a Christian perspective include: James Dobson, *Hide or Seek* (Old Tappan, NJ: Fleming H. Revell Co., 1974). H. Norman Wright, *The Christian Use of Emotional Power* (Old Tappan, NJ: Fleming H. Revell Co., 1974). Jo Berry, *Can You Love Yourself?* (Glendale, CA: Regal Books, 1978).

Notes for Chapter 14
1. Earl G. Lee, *Recycled for Living* (Glendale, CA: Regal Books, 1973), p. 4.
2. Lee, *Recycled for Living*, p. 6.
3. Lee, *Recycled for Living*, pp. 9,10.
4. Lee, *Recycled for Living*, p. 19.
5. Lee, *Recycled for Living*, p. 36.
6. See "You Pack Your Own Chute!" a 16-mm 30-minute color film starring Eden Ryle. Produced and distributed by Ramick Productions, 58 West 58th Street, New York, NY 10019. This film may be available in one of your local film libraries. It has been extensively used for training sessions in business and industry, government agencies, the military, hospitals, churches, penal institutions—even by Alcoholics Anonymous and Weight Watchers. A 24-page discussion guide is also available.

Notes for Chapter 15
1. Two out of every four marriages end in divorce: "The American Family: Can It Survive Today's Shocks?" *U.S. News and World Report* (October 27, 1975), p. 32.
2. William Barclay, *The Gospel of Matthew*, The Daily Study Bible (Edinburgh: The Saint Andrew Press, 1957), vol. 2, pp. 218,219.
3. D. Martyn Lloyd-Jones, *Studies in the Sermon on the Mount* (Grand Rapids: William B. Eerdmans Publishing Co., n.d.), vol. 1, pp. 254-257.

Notes for Chapter 16
1. Eric Berne, *Games People Play: The Psychology of Human Relationships* (New York: Grove Press, Inc., 1964), p. 88.
2. Rubin Carson, *The National Love, Sex and Marriage Test* (New York: Dolphin Books, 1978), p. 6.
3. Carson, *Marriage Test*, p. 2.

Notes for Chapter 17
1. Adapted from Dwight H. Small, *Marriage: Handle with Care* (Glendale, CA: Regal Books, 1977), p. 3.
2. Adapted from H. Norman Wright, *Communication: Key to Your Marriage* (Glendale, CA: Regal Books, 1974), p. 52.
3. Wright, *Communication*, pp. 163-166.

Helpful Resources on Marriage
Augsburger, David. *Caring Enough to Confront*. Glendale, CA: Regal Books, 1973.
Benson, Dan. *The Total Man*. Wheaton, IL: Tyndale House, 1977.
Dobson, James. *What Wives Wish Their Husbands Knew About Women*. Wheaton, IL: Tyndale House, 1975.
Foster, Timothy. *Dare to Lead*. Glendale, CA: Regal Books, 1977.
Guernsey, Dennis. *Thoroughly Married: Sexual Communication*. Waco, TX: Word Books, 1975.
LaHaye, Tim. *The Act of Marriage*. Grand Rapids: Zondervan Publishing House, 1977.
Lee, Mark. *Creative Christian Marriage*. Glendale, CA: Regal Books, 1977.
Merrill, Dean. *The Husband Book*. Grand Rapids: Zondervan Publishing House, 1977.
Shedd, Charlie. *Talk to Me!* Garden City, NY: Doubleday and Company, 1975.
Swihart, Judson. *How Do You Say "I Love You"?* Madison WI: Inter-Varsity Press, 1977.
Wright, H. Norman. *Communication: Key to Your Marriage*. Glendale, CA: Regal Books, 1974.
Yancy, Phillip. *After the Wedding*. Waco, TX: Word Books, 1977.

Notes for Chapter 18
1. William Barclay, *The Gospel According to Matthew*, The Daily Study Bible (Edinburgh: The Saint Andrew Press, 1957), vol. 2, p. 126.
2. Barclay, *Matthew*, vol. 2, pp. 127-129.

Notes for Chapter 19
1. Haim Ginott, *Between Parent and Child* (New York: Avon Books, 1969), p. xiii.
2. James Dobson, *Hide or Seek* (Old Tappan, NJ: Fleming H. Revell Company, 1974).

Notes for Chapter 20
1. In some churches, "honor thy father and mother" is the fifth commandment; while still other denominations make it the fourth.
2. Haim Ginott, *Between Parent and Child* (New York: Avon Books, 1969), p. 25.
3. Earl H. Gaulke, *You Can Have a Family Where Everybody Wins* (St. Louis: Concordia Press, 1975), p. 23.
4. William Barclay, *The Gospel According to Matthew*, The Daily Study Bible (Edinburgh: The Saint Andrew Press, 1957), vol. 2, pp. 212, 213.

Helpful Resources for Parents
Dobson, James. *Dare to Discipline*. Wheaton, IL: Tyndale House, 1970.
Dobson, James. *The Strong-Willed Child: Birth Through Adolescence*. Wheaton, IL: Tyndale House, 1978.
Narramore, Bruce. *Help—I'm a Parent!* Grand Rapids: Zondervan Publishing House, 1973.

Additional Helps for Parenting and Family Life

Dobson, James. *Hide or Seek.* Old Tappan, NJ: Fleming H. Revell, 1974.

Gangel, Kenneth. *The Family First.* Minneapolis: HIS International Service, 1972. Biblical answers to family problems.

Getz, Gene. *The Measure of a Family.* Glendale, CA: Regal Books, 1976.

Hendricks, Howard. *Heaven Help the Home.* Wheaton, IL: Victor Books, 1973.

Kesler, Jay. *I Want a Home with No Problems.* Waco, TX: Word Books, 1978.

Kesler, Jay. *Too Big to Spank.* Glendale, CA: Regal Books, 1978. Especially for parents of teenagers.

Narramore, Bruce. *An Ounce of Prevention.* Grand Rapids: Zondervan Publishing House, 1973.

Petersen, J. Allan, ed. *For Families Only: Answering the Tough Questions Parents Ask.* Wheaton IL: Tyndale House, 1977.

Richards, Larry. *You and Your Child.* Chicago, IL: Moody Press, 1974.

Rickerson, Wayne. *Getting Your Family Together.* Glendale, CA: Regal Books, 1977.

Rickerson, Wayne. *Good Times for Your Family.* Glendale, CA: Regal Books, 1976.

Scanzoni, Letha. *Sex Is a Parent Affair.* Glendale, CA: Regal Books, 1973.

Shedd, Charlie. *The Best Dad Is a Good Lover.* Kansas City: Shedd, Andrews and McMeel, Inc., 1977.

Wakefield, Norm. *You Can Have a Happier Family.* Glendale, CA: Regal Books, 1977.

Walker, Georgiana, ed. *The Celebration Book.* Glendale, CA: Regal Books, 1977.

Additional Helps for Active Listening

Gaulke, Earl H. *You Can Have a Family Where Everybody Wins.* St. Louis: Concordia Publishing House, 1975.

Gordon, Thomas. *Parent Effectiveness Training: The Tested New Way to Raise Responsible Children.* New York: Wyden, a Division of David McKay Co., 1977.

Notes for Chapter 21

1. D. Martyn Lloyd-Jones, *Studies in the Sermon on the Mount* (Grand Rapids: William B. Eerdmans Publishing Co., 1958), p. 58.

2. William Barclay, *The Gospel of Matthew,* The Daily Study Bible (Edinburgh: The Saint Andrew Press, 1959), vol. 2, p. 92.

3. Barclay, *Matthew,* vol. 2, p. 98.

4. Lloyd-Jones, *Studies in the Sermon on the Mount,* p. 104.

5. Lloyd-Jones, *Studies in the Sermon on the Mount,* pp. 109-110.

Notes for Chapter 23

1. Adapted from Edward R. Dayton and Ted W. Engstrom, *Strategy for Living* (Glendale, CA: Regal Books, 1976), p. 49.

2. Victor Frankl, *Man's Search for Meaning* (Boston: Beacon Press, 1959), p. 127.

3. Granted, if you are Jewish, the horrors of Hitler's holocaust do not seem remote. Many Jews—especially survivors of the Nazi activities in the 1940s, or close relatives of those who were murdered—were deeply moved or disturbed by the showing of "Holocaust" on NBC in April of 1978.